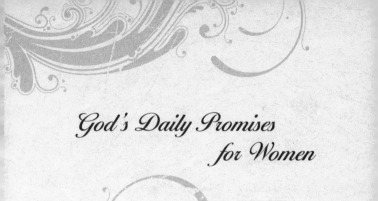

God's Daily Promises
for Women

D0188089

DAILY WISDOM
FROM GOD'S WORD

BOOKS IN THE
GOD'S DAILY PROMISES SERIES

God's Daily

PROMISES

for Women

DAILY WISDOM
FROM GOD'S WORD

Tyndale House Publishers, Inc.

Carol Stream, Illinois

Visit Tyndale's exciting Web site at www.tyndale.com

TYNDALE and Tyndale's quill logo are registered trademarks of Tyndale House Publishers, Inc.

New Living Translation, NLT, and the New Living Translation logo are registered trademarks of Tyndale House Publishers, Inc.

God's Daily Promises for Women: Daily Wisdom from God's Word

General Editors: Ron Beers and Amy Mason

Contributing Editor: Rebecca Beers

Contributing Writers: V. Gilbert Beers, Ronald A. Beers, Brian R. Coffey, Jonathan Farrar, Jonathan Gray, Shawn A. Harrison, Sandy Hull, Rhonda K. O'Brien, Douglas J. Rumford.

Designed by Julie Chen

Edited by Susan Taylor

ISBN-13: 978-1-4143-1231-6
ISBN-10: 1-4143-1231-8

Printed in the United States of America

13   12   11   10   09   08   07
 7   6   5   4   3   2   1

INTRODUCTION

Why did God make so many promises? Maybe it's
because he wants to show you how much you can
really trust him. Maybe he is so interested in you
that he is trying to get your attention with each amaz-
ing promise he makes, wanting to show you just
how much you have to look forward to as you travel
through life. This unique book presents more
than 365 of these incredible promises, at least one
for every day of the year. All these promises will
come true—or have already come true. You simply have to decide whether you want to be part of
them or not.

Imagine that every morning you could
be inspired by a promise from God's Word
and then live the rest of the day with either the
expectation that God will fulfill that promise
or the confidence that comes from a promise
already fulfilled. *God's Daily Promises for Women*
is designed to inspire you in just that way.
Every page is dated, making the book easy to
use. First, read the promise from God. Think
about it. Let it soak in. Then read the short
devotional note to help you look at your
day differently because of God's promise.
Finally, read the question at the end to
encourage and motivate you to trust that
this promise was meant for you. Claim the
promise as your own with the confidence

that you can always trust God to keep his word. Our prayer is that you will be blessed and encouraged as you see and experience all that God has in store for you.

—The Editors

JANUARY

BEGINNINGS

TODAY'S PROMISE

*Great is his faithfulness; his mercies begin afresh
each morning.* —LAMENTATIONS 3:23

TODAY'S THOUGHT

Life consists of a series of new beginnings; it's
your attitude toward them that makes all the difference. Each day provides new opportunities
for you to get to know God better and to start
over with new resolutions about how you will
respond to circumstances and people. God's
mercy is new every day, no matter what you've
done or how you've treated him the day before.
With God's forgiveness, you don't have to be bur-
dened by yesterday's failures or regrets.

TODAY'S PLAN

*Do you extend new mercies each day to the people you
love and live with, just as God extends new mercies to
you?*

TRANSFORMATION

TODAY'S PROMISE

I am certain that God, who began the good work within you, will continue his work until it is finally finished on the day when Christ Jesus returns.

—PHILIPPIANS 1:6

TODAY'S THOUGHT

From the minute God begins a "good work" in you, he promises to continue working in you for the rest of your life, transforming every aspect of your heart and your character. He will show you how to become more like him in your relationships, work, service, and love. If you ask him to work in you every day, you will be amazed at what you have become when he finally takes you home to be with him forever.

TODAY'S PLAN

What work does God need to do in you today? Are you open to his working in you?

GOALS

TODAY'S PROMISE

We can make our plans, but the Lord determines our steps. —PROVERBS 16:9

TODAY'S THOUGHT

Goals give you direction. You may have a lot of goals for different areas of life (including those New Year's resolutions you made), but following God should be your primary, overarching goal. You do not know what the year ahead will bring, but if the Lord determines your steps and you are following where he leads, you can be sure that your life will have purpose. In addition, when you keep your eyes on the goal, you will not stray from God, regardless of what difficulties you encounter.

TODAY'S PLAN

What kind of goal will it take to keep you following God closely each day?

CALL OF GOD

TODAY'S PROMISE

Don't copy the behavior and customs of this world, but let God transform you into a new person by changing the way you think. Then you will learn to know God's will for you, which is good and pleasing and perfect. —ROMANS 12:2

TODAY'S THOUGHT

When God is ready to call you to a specific task, he will keep interrupting your thoughts. Your heart will long to do what God wants you to do; you will know it is what you should do. Then opportunities to serve will follow. Seize the moment, and follow God's call. Don't let a window of opportunity close and miss all that God has in store for you as you follow his call.

TODAY'S PLAN

Are you listening for God's call to you?

DECISIONS

TODAY'S PROMISE

God loved the world so much that he gave his one and only Son, so that everyone who believes in him will not perish but have eternal life. —JOHN 3:16

TODAY'S THOUGHT

Despite the fact that change is a certainty in the world around you, you can always be truly secure about two things: First, when you make decisions and live each day based on the changeless truths of God's Word, you have complete assurance that you are doing the right thing. Second, when you have made the decision to follow Christ, who died and rose to give you new life, you can be absolutely sure that your eternal future with him in heaven is secure.

TODAY'S PLAN

Are you making sure that you are first making decisions about life's most important issues?

AFFIRMATION

TODAY'S PROMISE

God created human beings in his own image. In the image of God he created them; male and female he created them. —GENESIS 1:27

TODAY'S THOUGHT

When God created you, he affirmed you. He created you for a specific reason and purpose: to reflect his glory and characteristics. When you struggle with discouragement, remember how you have been created in God's likeness.

TODAY'S PLAN

Spend some time thinking about the qualities of God. You have many of these same qualities. Will you reflect them toward others?

GUIDANCE

TODAY'S PROMISE

We can make our plans, but the Lord determines our steps. —PROVERBS 16:9

Trust in the Lord with all your heart; do not depend on your own understanding. Seek his will in all you do, and he will show you which path to take.

—PROVERBS 3:5-6

TODAY'S THOUGHT

God's guidance is less like a searchlight, which brightens a wide area, and more like a flashlight, which illuminates just enough of the path ahead to show you where to take the next few steps. God has a definite plan for you. Never doubt that. But he usually doesn't reveal it all at once. He wants you to learn to trust him each step of the way.

TODAY'S PLAN

Where is God asking you to trust his guidance today?

GOALS

All of you should be of one mind. Sympathize with each other. Love each other as brothers and sisters. Be tenderhearted, and keep a humble attitude. Don't repay evil for evil. Don't retaliate with insults when people insult you. Instead, pay them back with a blessing. —1 PETER 3:8-9

TODAY'S THOUGHT

Although it's good to have big goals, it's also important to set smaller daily goals. Being kind and humble toward others, doing good when someone takes advantage of you, reading your Bible, or offering encouragement may seem to be small goals when compared with loftier ones, but they become the essential building blocks of all that God wants you to accomplish.

TODAY'S PLAN

What "small" goals can you set for yourself today?

COPING

Seek his will in all you do, and he will show you which path to take. —PROVERBS 3:6

Seek the Kingdom of God above all else, and live righteously, and he will give you everything you need. —MATTHEW 6:33

TODAY'S THOUGHT

When life seems overwhelming, what can help you to cope with the stress of living in a culture that tends to view busyness as something to be admired? The key is to set your priorities early. If you make time with God and his Word your first priority, you will gain a godly perspective on your activities for the rest of the day.

TODAY'S PLAN

Is God first on your daily agenda?

PRAYER

TODAY'S PROMISE

I love the Lord because he hears my voice and my prayer for mercy. Because he bends down to listen, I will pray as long as I have breath! —PSALM 116:1-2

TODAY'S THOUGHT

God listens carefully to every prayer and answers it. His response may be yes, no, or wait, the same way any loving parent would respond to a child. Answering yes to every request would spoil you and be dangerous to your well-being. Answering no to every request would be vindictive and stingy and would kill your spirit. Answering wait to every prayer would be frustrating. God always answers based on what he knows is best for you. When you don't get the answer you want, you will grow in spiritual maturity as you try to understand why God's answer is in your best interest.

TODAY'S PLAN

How can you be more spiritually sensitive to recognize God's answer to each of your prayers?

FUTURE

TODAY'S PROMISE

"I know the plans I have for you," says the LORD. "They are plans for good and not for disaster, to give you a future and a hope." —JEREMIAH 29:11

TODAY'S THOUGHT

God directs your steps. He knows what you will encounter on the road of life, and only he can direct you in the best way for you to go. Though the pathway may lead through some dark valleys or seem to take some unnecessary detours, someday you will look back on those twists and turns and discover that God's way was best. God finishes what he starts. Don't allow your limitations or your present difficulties to blind you to the truth that your present insecurities are opportunities for God's work in your heart. As long as God has work for you to do, he will guide you to where you need to be.

TODAY'S PLAN

Are you prepared to let God work out his plan and purpose for your life?

BEGINNINGS

TODAY'S PROMISE

Anyone who belongs to Christ has become a new person. The old life is gone; a new life has begun!

—2 CORINTHIANS 5:17

TODAY'S THOUGHT

Do you ever long for a fresh start? When you place your faith in Jesus, you get a new beginning because his forgiveness washes your sins away and gives you a clean, new heart. Then God puts his Holy Spirit in your clean heart and gives you the strength, power, and wisdom to live the way God created you to live. When you do mess up, God's forgiveness always provides the opportunity to begin again, any day and anytime.

TODAY'S PLAN

Do you need a fresh start?

PASSION

TODAY'S PROMISE

I will give them singleness of heart and put a new spirit within them. I will take away their stony, stubborn heart and give them a tender, responsive heart.

—EZEKIEL 11:19

TODAY'S THOUGHT

Is there some need that is constantly moving your heart? a ministry you feel drawn to? a cause you can't stop thinking about? If so, this deep yearning is a passion that God has put inside you, a direction he may be calling you to go. If you don't feel this way about anything, ask God to soften your heart toward those he wants you to serve, and to give you a passion for seeing and meeting a need.

TODAY'S PLAN

Is God stirring a particular passion inside you?

PATIENCE

TODAY'S PROMISE

You are my strength; I wait for you to rescue me, for you, O God, are my fortress. —PSALM 59:9

TODAY'S THOUGHT

The only way to develop patience is to be in a position where you need it. You may find yourself in a situation that never seems to change because God wants you to learn to trust him in the meantime. God will change your situation when he's ready, and when he *is* ready, the timing will be best for you, too. Your time "on hold," waiting to be rescued, is not wasted if you are serving God right where you are.

TODAY'S PLAN

What is God asking you to wait for?

JANUARY 15

ASSURANCE

Through Christ you have come to trust in God. And you have placed your faith and hope in God because he raised Christ from the dead and gave him great glory. —1 PETER 1:21

Trust is essential in a good relationship. If you trust someone, you can be sure of him or her. But only God can be trusted completely without fear of disappointment. People, who are not perfect, will sometimes fail you; God, who is perfect, will never fail you. The world is filled with uncertainty, but you can have complete assurance that God will keep his promises.

How does the knowledge that he will keep those promises affect your relationship with him today?

PAIN

TODAY'S PROMISE

He will wipe every tear from their eyes, and there will be no more death or sorrow or crying or pain. All these things are gone forever. —REVELATION 21:4

TODAY'S THOUGHT

Whether it comes from betrayal, neglect, or abandonment or a broken bone or failing health—the result is emotional or physical pain. You may remember the physical pain of an illness or the chest-tightening pang that comes from a broken heart. Your greatest source of hope in such times is God's healing power. Although God does not promise to remove your pain in this life, he does promise to be with you through it and give you hope and purpose in the seeming despair of your aching body and soul. Most important, God promises to remove your pain forever in eternity.

TODAY'S PLAN

Can your hope of a pain-free eternity help you to bear your pain now?

COMMITMENT

TODAY'S PROMISE

Trust in the LORD with all your heart; do not depend on your own understanding. Seek his will in all you do, and he will show you which path to take.

—PROVERBS 3:5-6

TODAY'S THOUGHT

Trusting God with all your heart means resolving to obey God and to let him show you how to live in all areas of your life. As a human being with a sinful nature, you will never be able to completely achieve this goal in this life, but don't let that keep you from a commitment to do your best. As you trust God and seek his will, he will direct you to the people, places, and opportunities that he knows will give your life purpose and satisfaction.

TODAY'S PLAN

On a scale of one to ten, how committed are you to trusting God?

WILL OF GOD

TODAY'S PROMISE

Keep on asking, and you will receive what you ask for. Keep on seeking, and you will find. Keep on knocking, and the door will be opened to you. For everyone who asks, receives. Everyone who seeks, finds. And to everyone who knocks, the door will be opened.

—MATTHEW 7:7-8

TODAY'S THOUGHT

God's work will get done, if not by you then by someone else. If you want to participate in God's will, you can't sit around waiting for God to write a message on your wall. You have a choice about whether you will be participating in God's will or not. Seek his guidance first, and then make a decision to move ahead. If your choices always involve asking God for guidance, they will usually be in line with his will, and you will have the privilege of being involved in his work.

TODAY'S PLAN

Will you seek God's wisdom and then do what you believe he is asking you to do in accomplishing his will?

NEW NATURE

TODAY'S PROMISE

Wisdom is sweet to your soul. If you find it, you will have a bright future, and your hopes will not be cut short.
—PROVERBS 24:14

The Spirit who lives in you is greater than the spirit who lives in the world.
—1 JOHN 4:4

TODAY'S THOUGHT

You can't be truly wise on your own; you need God's wisdom. You can't be truly good or honest or peace loving on your own without being changed from the inside. You were born with a sinful nature—a desire and tendency to sin and do wrong. When you ask God to change your life, his Spirit lives in you and helps you overcome your sinful desires. You can be good and honest and peace loving because the Spirit is living in you.

TODAY'S PLAN

Have you asked God's Spirit to live in you and make you the person he wants you to be?

DOUBT

TODAY'S PROMISE

When doubts filled my mind, your comfort gave me renewed hope and cheer. —PSALM 94:19

TODAY'S THOUGHT

Virtually every biblical hero struggled with doubts about God and his ability or desire to help. God doesn't mind doubt as long as you keep searching for answers from him. But doubt can become sin if it leads you away from God to skepticism to cynicism and then to hard-heartedness. But God promises that doubt will become a blessing when your honest searching leads you to a better understanding of who he is and to a deeper faith in him. When others see your confidence in God as you struggle with doubt, they will be inspired to follow your example and to cling to their faith in God in all circumstances.

TODAY'S PLAN

When you find yourself doubting God, how will you respond?

FAILURE

TODAY'S PROMISE

Each time [the Lord] said, "My grace is all you need. My power works best in weakness."

—2 CORINTHIANS 12:9

TODAY'S THOUGHT

One thing is certain: You must learn to live with failure. In fact, you can embrace it, because it is through your failure that God's power works best in you. Everyone has weaknesses. Everyone fails—a lot. The key to success is not in how little you fail but in how you respond when you do. Those who admit their failures and look forward to an extra measure of God's strength to help them through it will go on to accomplish great things.

TODAY'S PLAN

The next time you fail, how can you look forward to God's releasing more of his power through you?

MEDITATION

TODAY'S PROMISE

I wait quietly before God, for my victory comes from him. . . . Let all that I am wait quietly before God, for my hope is in him. —PSALM 62:1, 5

TODAY'S THOUGHT

Meditation is intentionally thinking about God, talking to him and listening to him. When you make the time to really listen to God, you remove yourself from the distractions and noise of the world. You prepare yourself to be taught and to have your desires molded into what God desires. As a result, you will change, and your thoughts and actions will fall more in line with his will. Meditation goes beyond the study of God to communion with him, and that ultimately leads to godly actions.

TODAY'S PLAN

How can you make meditation with God more of a daily habit?

FRIENDSHIP

TODAY'S PROMISE

We can rejoice in our wonderful new relationship with God because our Lord Jesus Christ has made us friends of God. —ROMANS 5:11

TODAY'S THOUGHT

Does it seem strange to think of being friends with the God of the universe, especially since you can't see or touch him in a physical way? It might help you to consider what qualities make friendships strong: time, communication, honesty, loyalty. Friendship with God involves these same qualities. You can experience the joys of friendship with God if you truly want to know him better, listen to him, be loyal to him, and love him.

TODAY'S PLAN

In what ways can you demonstrate the qualities of good friendship in your relationship with God?

VALUE

TODAY'S PROMISE

Listen to the LORD who created you. . . . The one who formed you says, "Do not be afraid, for I have ransomed you. I have called you by name; you are mine. . . . You are precious to me. You are honored, and I love you." —ISAIAH 43:1, 4

TODAY'S THOUGHT

You are of such value to God that he not only created you in his image and made you unique, but his Spirit also works inside you. The God of the universe loves you and wants you to live with him now and forever. He promises that if you belong to him, you will be his forever, and his love for you will never die.

TODAY'S PLAN

Are you having a hard time accepting how valuable you are to God?

DEPRESSION

TODAY'S PROMISE

Even in darkness I cannot hide from you. To you the night shines as bright as day. Darkness and light are the same to you. —PSALM 139:12

TODAY'S THOUGHT

Jesus understands what it feels like to have your soul crushed to the point of death and to experience the "dark night of the soul." When you feel this low, it's hard to have any sense of hope. However, the darkness of depression doesn't have to block out the light of God's healing. Cry out to him from your darkness. He will hear and comfort you, hold you close, and begin to heal you. He will not let you go. In his timing and with his guidance, you will become stronger and eventually able to be a blessing to others in need.

TODAY'S PLAN

Do you feel your depression hides you from God's blessings? What would it take for his light to shine into your darkness?

CONTENTMENT

TODAY'S PROMISE

God blesses those who are poor and realize their need for him, for the Kingdom of Heaven is theirs.

—MATTHEW 5:3

TODAY'S THOUGHT

When you realize your need for God, you begin to understand how spiritually poor you are without him and that only he can meet your deepest needs. The Bible teaches that contentment and joy do not come from the pursuit of happiness, pleasure, or material wealth but from the pursuit of an intimate relationship with God. The harder you focus on pleasing yourself, the more discontented you will feel. The more you focus on pleasing God, the more contented you will be.

TODAY'S PLAN

What do you pursue in hopes of finding contentment?

FREEDOM

TODAY'S PROMISE

The LORD God warned him, "You may freely eat the fruit of every tree in the garden—except the tree of the knowledge of good and evil. If you eat its fruit, you are sure to die." —GENESIS 2:16-17

TODAY'S THOUGHT

Genuine love requires the freedom to choose. From the beginning, God desired a loving relationship with you, so he gave you this freedom. But with the ability to make choices comes the possibility of choosing your own way over God's way. Sin and evil exist because God's creatures have chosen their own way instead of God's. But you can choose to do what is right. You can choose God's way. And when you do, God is greatly pleased and rewards you.

TODAY'S PLAN

What will you do today with your freedom to choose?

HAPPINESS

TODAY'S PROMISE

The LORD your God will delight in you if you obey his voice and keep the commands and decrees written in this Book of Instruction, and if you turn to the LORD your God with all your heart and soul.

—DEUTERONOMY 30:10

TODAY'S THOUGHT

Can finite, sinful human beings truly bring joy and delight to the Lord, the Creator of the universe? Yes. God created you because he *wants* to have a relationship with you, to delight in being with you. When you do the things that please God, he takes delight in you. By loving and obeying God wholeheartedly, you put yourself in the position to become all that God created you to be. The only way to find happiness that lasts a lifetime is to commit yourself to pleasing God.

TODAY'S PLAN

How can you approach this day knowing that God delights in you?

BACKSLIDING

TODAY'S PROMISE

Everyone has sinned; we all fall short of God's glorious standard. Yet God, with undeserved kindness, declares that we are righteous. He did this through Christ Jesus when he freed us from the penalty for our sins.　—ROMANS 3:23-24

TODAY'S THOUGHT

It will happen to you as it does to almost everyone from time to time. You'll suddenly realize you are farther from God than you should be. It worries you, maybe scares you. Don't ignore that internal warning. Find out what happened— was it the result of simple neglect, or was it the consequence of a sinful habit that you don't want to give up? Only when you recognize what you've done can you confess it to God, and only by confessing can you be forgiven and begin the process of restoring your relationship with him.

TODAY'S PLAN

Today, will you move closer to God or farther from him?

EMPTINESS

TODAY'S PROMISE

[God] saved us, not because of the righteous things we had done, but because of his mercy. He washed away our sins, giving us a new birth and new life through the Holy Spirit. He generously poured out the Spirit upon us through Jesus Christ our Savior.

—TITUS 3:5-6

TODAY'S THOUGHT

When you accept God's gift of salvation and believe that Jesus Christ is your Savior, you are filled with his Holy Spirit. Along with God's love, help, encouragement, peace, and comfort, his presence goes with you. If you are not filled with God's Holy Spirit, your heart is like an empty house waiting to be occupied. Satan is looking for empty hearts to fill with his presence. Don't allow him to occupy your heart.

TODAY'S PLAN

How are you filling the emptiness in your heart?

CONFESSION

TODAY'S PROMISE

Everyone who believes in [Jesus] will have their sins forgiven through his name. —ACTS 10:43

TODAY'S THOUGHT

When you confess your sin, you agree with God that something wrong needs to be made right and that a broken relationship needs to be restored. Confession is the act of recognizing your sins before God so he can forgive you. Sin separates you from a holy God; confession communicates your desire to be in a right relationship with him. God promises that those who confess their sins to him will be forgiven. This gives you the freedom to have a relationship with Almighty God.

TODAY'S PLAN

How might your life change if you confessed your sins to God and received his forgiveness today? Can you imagine a close relationship with the God of the universe?

FEBRUARY

POTENTIAL

TODAY'S PROMISE

[God said,] "You must go wherever I send you and say whatever I tell you. And don't be afraid . . . for I will be with you and will protect you. I, the LORD, have spoken!" —JEREMIAH 1:6-8

TODAY'S THOUGHT

God promises to be with you when you follow wherever he leads you. And when he is with you, he will make sure you reach your God-given potential.

TODAY'S PLAN

Are you following God closely? If so, he will lead you to the place where you will fulfill your greatest potential.

CHALLENGES

TODAY'S PROMISE

In your strength I can crush an army; with my God I can scale any wall. —2 SAMUEL 22:30

TODAY'S THOUGHT

For most of us, every day brings some kind of challenge. We may not rule nations or run large corporations, but we face tough situations, difficult people, and temptations. Challenges keep us from becoming too comfortable and satisfied with the status quo; they force us to follow God's leading into uncharted waters. Without God, this kind of challenge can be frightening, but *with* God it can be a great adventure. Whatever challenge you face, make sure that you face it with God at your side.

TODAY'S PLAN

What is holding you back from confronting a challenge you are facing right now? If you picture God by your side, can you move forward with more confidence?

GENEROSITY

TODAY'S PROMISE

Share your food with the hungry, and give shelter to the homeless. Give clothes to those who need them, and do not hide from relatives who need your help.

—ISAIAH 58:7

TODAY'S THOUGHT

Generosity flows from a heart that understands that it is indebted to the love of God. God calls you to bring his love and grace to those in your circle of influence, always being willing to give something to help those in need. Your generous nature not only encourages and strengthens those around you but is also an expression of your gratefulness for what God has done for you. As a reward, God gives you more of his perfect character, he more directly guides your way, and he protects you from spiritual harm.

TODAY'S PLAN

Who desperately needs your help today? Who needs to receive God's love flowing through your heart and hands?

DIVERSITY

TODAY'S PROMISE

We are many parts of one body, and we all belong to each other. In his grace, God has given us different gifts for doing certain things well. —ROMANS 12:5-6

TODAY'S THOUGHT

Just as all kinds of instruments strengthen an orchestra, so people with different gifts and different perspectives make a team stronger. You have a gift that God has given specifically to you so that you can do something well for his Kingdom work. God puts people with different gifts together so that the various gifts can complement each other. It is ironic that through diversity God's Kingdom makes the most progress.

TODAY'S PLAN

Have you discovered the gift God has given you? Have you learned how your unique gift is different from those of others around you and yet equally important?

ADVERSITY

TODAY'S PROMISE

When troubles come your way, consider it an
opportunity for great joy. For you know that when
your faith is tested, your endurance has a chance
to grow.
                                                —JAMES 1:2-3

TODAY'S THOUGHT

One thing you can count on is that you will
experience adversity. The issue is what you will
do with it. Although it's hard to understand
adversity, there are benefits from experiencing
adversity. If God didn't build up your ability to
withstand adversity, you would crumble under
it. When adversity comes, move quickly toward
God, and keep your focus on him. Then you will
develop the strength to overcome.

TODAY'S PLAN

Are you experiencing some form of adversity now? How
might God be strengthening you through it?

PURPOSE

TODAY'S PROMISE

You made all the delicate, inner parts of my body and knit me together in my mother's womb. . . . You saw me before I was born. Every day of my life was recorded in your book. Every moment was laid out before a single day had passed. —PSALM 139:13, 16

TODAY'S THOUGHT

God has both general and specific purposes for you. Generally speaking, God wants you to let the love of Jesus shine through you to have an impact on others. More specifically, God has given you spiritual gifts and wants you to use them to make a unique contribution in your sphere of influence. The more you fulfill your general purpose, the more clear your specific purpose will become.

TODAY'S PLAN

Are you fulfilling your purpose of living according to God's Word and letting Jesus' love shine through you?

BROKEN HEART

TODAY'S PROMISE

The LORD is close to the brokenhearted; he rescues those whose spirits are crushed. —PSALM 34:18

TODAY'S THOUGHT

God promises that he is never far from you when your heart is breaking. He is a God of compassion who is always ready to help his loved ones. When your heart is broken, so is his.

TODAY'S PLAN

Can you picture God's heart breaking with yours? If you can, you will find great comfort when you stay close to him.

WISDOM

TODAY'S PROMISE

If you need wisdom, ask our generous God, and he will give it to you. He will not rebuke you for asking. But when you ask him, be sure that your faith is in God alone. Do not waver, for a person with divided loyalty is as unsettled as a wave of the sea that is blown and tossed by the wind. —JAMES 1:5-6

TODAY'S THOUGHT

God's Word consistently invites you to ask for the wisdom and direction you need. With all the people and circumstances that depend on you, it is imperative that you continually seek God's counsel, for who is wiser then he? God is pleased with those who ask him for wisdom because he has the information you are looking for, he wants what is best for you, and he delights in advising those who consult him.

TODAY'S PLAN

Where is the first place you go when you need advice? How could you develop the habit of first turning to God?

LOYALTY

TODAY'S PROMISE

The LORD leads with unfailing love and faithfulness all who keep his covenant and obey his demands.

—PSALM 25:10

TODAY'S THOUGHT

Loyalty can be defined as a highly personal form of commitment. Loyalty says, "No matter what happens around us or between us, no fear, doubt, or hurt can make me turn my back on you." When loyalty is present, a relationship is secure and solid. When it is not, you live in insecurity and fear. The Bible teaches that loyalty is part of the character of God himself. He expresses his loyalty by refusing to give up on you no matter how often you disappoint him. You express your loyalty to God through obedience to his Word.

TODAY'S PLAN

How loyal are you to God? Are you modeling this same loyalty to those you love?

ATTITUDE

TODAY'S PROMISE

A peaceful heart leads to a healthy body; jealousy is like cancer in the bones. —PROVERBS 14:30

A cheerful heart is good medicine, but a broken spirit saps a person's strength. —PROVERBS 17:22

TODAY'S THOUGHT

Attitude makes all the difference. Faith is an attitude that believes events in your life happen under God's direction rather than randomly. This allows you to view your life from a perspective of hope rather than defeat. It allows you to be positive about circumstances rather than negative, because you know God will take whatever happens and bring good from it.

TODAY'S PLAN

Is it time for an attitude check?

HEART

TODAY'S PROMISE

Teach me your ways, O LORD, that I may live according to your truth! Grant me purity of heart, so that I may honor you. —PSALM 86:11

TODAY'S THOUGHT

You harvest what you plant. Pumpkin seeds produce pumpkins. Sunflower seeds produce sunflowers. If bad desires and thoughts remain in your heart, it is evidence that some bad seeds got planted and you need to do some weeding. Ask the Lord to plant a pure and obedient spirit in your heart so that your life will be characterized by clean thoughts, actions, and motives.

TODAY'S PLAN

What might you look like a year from now—inside and outside—if you pursued purity of heart? How can you start today?

FAITHFULNESS

TODAY'S PROMISE

If we are unfaithful, he remains faithful, for he cannot deny who he is. —2 TIMOTHY 2:13

TODAY'S THOUGHT

Who are you really—deep down inside? Do you really love others? Are you really faithful to your family, friends, and coworkers? Faithfulness is necessary if you are to maintain love, because even those closest to you will disappoint you at times. Despite your sin, God loves you and remains faithful to you. Model that same love to others, and remain faithful to them, even when they fail you. Then your love will be genuine, and others will know you truly care.

TODAY'S PLAN

How are you passing the test of faithfulness?

LOVE

TODAY'S PROMISE

God showed how much he loved us by sending his one and only Son into the world so that we might have eternal life through him. This is real love—not that we loved God, but that he loved us and sent his Son as a sacrifice to take away our sins. —1 JOHN 4:9-10

TODAY'S THOUGHT

One of the greatest expressions of love is sacrifice. God gave up his own son, Jesus, as an expression of his love for you. This is real, unconditional love. As you think about your most important relationships, do you love others based on how much they love you, or do you love unconditionally, regardless of how others treat you?

TODAY'S PLAN

What would your relationship with God be like if he put conditions on his love for you?

LOVE

TODAY'S PROMISE

Love is patient and kind. Love is not jealous or boastful or proud or rude. It does not demand its own way. It is not irritable, and it keeps no record of being wronged. It does not rejoice about injustice but rejoices whenever the truth wins out. Love never gives up, never loses faith, is always hopeful, and endures through every circumstance. . . . Three things will last forever—faith, hope, and love—and the greatest of these is love. —1 CORINTHIANS 13:4-7, 13

TODAY'S THOUGHT

Love is the greatest of all human qualities, and it is an attribute of God himself. Love involves unselfish service to others, which is the evidence that you truly care, whether or not someone cares in return. Faith is the foundation and content of God's message; hope is the attitude and focus; but love is the action. Love proves that your faith and hope are genuine.

TODAY'S PLAN

To whom can you show love today?

LOVE OF GOD

TODAY'S PROMISE

The LORD says, "I will rescue those who love me. I will protect those who trust in my name. When they call on me, I will answer; I will be with them in trouble. I will rescue and honor them. I will reward them with a long life and give them my salvation."

—PSALM 91:14-16

TODAY'S THOUGHT

God loves you because he made you. You are not a random creature evolved from a primordial soup. God created you in his own image to have a relationship with him and to bring him glory. He desires your friendship, and he is courting you now. Pursue him, and discover the purpose for which you were made.

TODAY'S PLAN

Are you responding to God's loving pursuit, or are you running from him?

FAITH

TODAY'S PROMISE

Faith comes from hearing, that is, hearing the Good News about Christ. —ROMANS 10:17

TODAY'S THOUGHT

Faith is not simply a matter of positive thinking or human effort. Faith is inspired by the Holy Spirit working through the Word of God to transform the way you think and act. When you absorb God's Word into your mind and heart, it becomes part of you. Your faith will strengthen as you read the Bible and reflect on its words about who God is, his guidelines for living, and how he wants to work on earth through you. God's gift of faith grows as you read how God has worked through people across the centuries and then realize that he will do the same in you.

TODAY'S PLAN

Are you using the truth of God's Word to strengthen your faith?

COMFORT

TODAY'S PROMISE

He comforts us in all our troubles so that we can comfort others. When they are troubled, we will be able to give them the same comfort God has given us.

—2 CORINTHIANS 1:4

TODAY'S THOUGHT

God promises to comfort you in times of trouble and grief, not just so you will feel his comfort, but also so that you will be better equipped to comfort others in their hardships. God does most of his work through people, so his comfort often comes through others to you. Then God wants his comfort to flow through you to others. As you share your experiences of God's comfort, others will find it as well.

TODAY'S PLAN

Is God's comfort reaching you? Are you passing it on to others?

PURITY

TODAY'S PROMISE

Wash me clean from my guilt. Purify me from my sin. . . . Purify me from my sins, and I will be clean; wash me, and I will be whiter than snow.

—PSALM 51:2, 7

TODAY'S THOUGHT

One dead fly in a pitcher of ice water contaminates the whole thing. It is not enough to merely remove the fly; you have to dump out the contaminated water and fill a new pitcher with clean water. In the same way, mixing sin into your life contaminates your relationship with God and with others and causes you to become spiritually polluted. But Jesus' death on the cross purified your contaminated life so that you could be pure and clean in God's presence—something you could not do on your own. God's forgiveness is like an endless spring of pure water. When you humbly ask God to forgive you, he removes the contamination and makes you fresh and pure again.

TODAY'S PLAN

How much is sin contaminating you?

DESIRES

TODAY'S PROMISE

I will give you a new heart, and I will put a new spirit in you. I will take out your stony, stubborn heart and give you a tender, responsive heart.

—EZEKIEL 36:26

TODAY'S THOUGHT

When you commit your life to God, he gives you a new heart, a new nature, and a new desire to please him. When God stirs your heart, your desires will be in line with his, which means that what you want to do will be what he wants you to do. Your will is going to be God's will for you. There is nothing more wonderful than having your desires match God's.

TODAY'S PLAN

Are you taking full advantage of the new heart God has given you? How?

FORGIVENESS

TODAY'S PROMISE

He does not punish us for all our sins; he does not deal harshly with us, as we deserve. For his unfailing love toward those who fear him is as great as the height of the heavens above the earth. He has removed our sins as far from us as the east is from the west. —PSALM 103:10-12

TODAY'S THOUGHT

Forgiveness requires two parties: one to ask for it and the other to grant it. Between you and God, you are always on the asking side, and he is always on the giving side. If you are sincere, you are assured of God's forgiveness because he has more than enough love and mercy to give. No matter what mistakes you've made, when you belong to Jesus, God promises to take the stain of your sin and completely remove it.

TODAY'S PLAN

Have you been a recipient of God's forgiveness?

OBEDIENCE

TODAY'S PROMISE

Do what is right and good in the LORD's sight, so all will go well with you. —DEUTERONOMY 6:18

TODAY'S THOUGHT

The right thing to do is the smart thing to do. God's commandments are not burdensome obligations; they are pathways to joyful, meaningful, satisfying lives. God's call for your obedience is based on his own commitment to your well-being. Since God is the Creator of life, he knows how life is supposed to work and what is best for you. Obedience demonstrates your willingness to follow through on what he says is best and to trust that God's way will work for you.

TODAY'S PLAN

Do you see obedience as a pathway to the best for your life or as a burdensome obligation?

ABILITIES

TODAY'S PROMISE

Now these . . . gifts Christ gave to the church . . . to equip God's people to do his work and build up the church, the body of Christ . . . until we all come to such unity in our faith and knowledge of God's Son that we will be mature in the Lord, measuring up to the full and complete standard of Christ.

—EPHESIANS 4:11-13

TODAY'S THOUGHT

You will feel happier and more fulfilled when you use your God-given abilities. So rejoice in your abilities, but let that rejoicing be poured in thanks to the God who gave them. Without God, your abilities are dreams without power, cups without water, engines without fuel.

TODAY'S PLAN

Are you gratefully using the abilities God has given you?

LONELINESS

TODAY'S PROMISE

Nothing can ever separate us from God's love. Neither death nor life, neither angels nor demons, neither our fears for today nor our worries about tomorrow—not even the powers of hell can separate us from God's love. No power in the sky above or in the earth below—indeed, nothing in all creation will ever be able to separate us from the love of God.

—ROMANS 8:38-39

TODAY'S THOUGHT

Have you ever felt desperately alone and rejected? Perhaps a best friend deserted you, the marriage you hoped for never happened, or the person you did marry wants out. Ironically, you can feel equally lonely on a crowded city street or in a busy airport. But God's promise to the lonely is "Do not be afraid, for I am with you" (Isaiah 43:5).

TODAY'S PLAN

Are you cultivating a friendship with God?

GRIEF

TODAY'S PROMISE

The Holy Spirit helps us in our weakness. For example, we don't know what God wants us to pray for. But the Holy Spirit prays for us with groanings that cannot be expressed in words. And the Father who knows all hearts knows what the Spirit is saying, for the Spirit pleads for us believers in harmony with God's own will. —ROMANS 8:26-27

TODAY'S THOUGHT

When you are in such confusion that you don't even know how to express your feelings to God, the Holy Spirit prays and expresses them for you. When you are unable to form the words of your prayer, let the Holy Spirit intercede for you. When you can't pray for yourself, the Spirit can pray for you and implore God to give you the comfort and guidance you so desperately need.

TODAY'S PLAN

How can it comfort you to know the Holy Spirit of God is praying for you?

CONFLICT

TODAY'S PROMISE

Live in harmony and peace. Then the God of love and peace will be with you. —2 CORINTHIANS 13:11

TODAY'S THOUGHT

Living in peace with others does not mean avoiding conflict but rather handling conflict appropriately. Conflict handled poorly leads to fractured relationships. Avoiding conflict altogether can have the same result because there is unresolved hurt and anger. God promises to be with those who work for peace and harmony with others because they are striving for the qualities God says are essential to relationships with others and to a relationship with him.

TODAY'S PLAN

Are you seeking the kind of peace that doesn't avoid conflict but rather ends it?

HELP

TODAY'S PROMISE

The LORD is my strength and shield. I trust him with all my heart. He helps me, and my heart is filled with joy. I burst out in songs of thanksgiving.

—PSALM 28:7

TODAY'S THOUGHT

If you focus on trying to get *yourself* out of trouble, you will never see what God can do. God loves to help and encourage those who depend on him and trust him completely. When you ask God to help you, and trust that he will, you open the lifeline to the God who loves doing the impossible, and you change your focus from panic to joy.

TODAY'S PLAN

Where do you need help? Are you ready to see what God can do?

BUILDING UP OTHERS

TODAY'S PROMISE

Be joyful. Grow to maturity. Encourage each other. Live in harmony and peace. Then the God of love and peace will be with you. —2 CORINTHIANS 13:11

TODAY'S THOUGHT

Why does God promise to be with those who build others up? Maybe it's because building up others affirms the gifts God has placed in them and helps others fulfill the purpose for which they were created. When you play a role in helping to release God's gifts in others by building them up, God wants to help you in every way he can.

TODAY'S PLAN

Is there someone you can build up today?

EXCUSES

TODAY'S PROMISE

"LORD," Gideon replied, "how can I rescue Israel? My clan is the weakest in the whole tribe of Manasseh, and I am the least in my entire family!" The LORD said to him, "I will be with you."

—JUDGES 6:15-16

TODAY'S THOUGHT

Gideon thought he had a good excuse for not serving God, but the qualifications God looks for are different from what we might expect. He often chooses the least likely people to do his work in order to more effectively demonstrate his power. If you know God has called you to do something, stop trying to excuse yourself. He promises to give you the help and strength you need to get the job done.

TODAY'S PLAN

Are you making excuses to get out of something God wants you to do?

DEPRESSION

TODAY'S PROMISE

Even in darkness I cannot hide from you. To you the night shines as bright as day. Darkness and light are the same to you. —PSALM 139:12

TODAY'S THOUGHT

Jesus understands what it feels like to have your soul crushed to the point of death and to live through "the dark night of the soul." When you feel this low, you feel hopeless. However, the darkness of depression doesn't have to block out the light of God's healing. Cry out to him even from your darkness. He will hear and comfort you, hold you, and begin to heal you. In time, you will become stronger and eventually able to be a blessing to others in need.

TODAY'S PLAN

Do you feel your depression hides you from God's blessing? What would it take for his light to shine into your darkness?

MARCH

CHARACTER

TODAY'S PROMISE

The more you grow like this, the more productive and useful you will be in your knowledge of our Lord Jesus Christ.

—2 PETER 1:8

TODAY'S THOUGHT

Character is what you are, but it is also what you desire to become. Ultimately, your character determines the mark you leave on society. Those who strive for godly character work toward moral excellence. We work hard all our lives to become excellent in many areas, especially in the areas of job and hobbies, so it makes sense to also work hard at becoming morally excellent, to be known as someone who has mastered the art of living in areas that really matter, like integrity, kindness, love, and faithfulness. You master these skills by asking God's Spirit to work through you—to be your hands and feet—as you relate to others.

TODAY'S PLAN

Your reputation—what other people are saying about you—is often a good indicator of your character. If two people were talking about you, what would they say?

TEMPTATION

The temptations in your life are no different from what others experience. And God is faithful. He will not allow the temptation to be more than you can stand. When you are tempted, he will show you a way out so that you can endure. —1 CORINTHIANS 10:13

TODAY'S THOUGHT

God's Word makes it clear that sin always hurts you because it separates you from God (the source of mercy and blessing) and puts you within reach of the enemy. Giving in to temptation puts you right in the middle of the road, where evil hurtles toward you at high speed. God has promised to give you the strength to resist temptation. The next time you find yourself moving toward something you know is wrong, get off the road of temptation before the consequences of sin run you over.

TODAY'S PLAN

Where are you most vulnerable to temptation?

BITTERNESS

TODAY'S PROMISE

Look after each other so that none of you fails to receive the grace of God. Watch out that no poisonous root of bitterness grows up to trouble you, corrupting many.
—HEBREWS 12:15

TODAY'S THOUGHT

Forgiveness is the antidote to bitterness. It lifts burdens, cancels debts, and frees you from the chains of unresolved anger. Holding grudges and being resentful spread ugly rumors and attitudes that negatively affect those around you. Forgiveness frees you from having to judge others and spreads an attitude of love, care, and acceptance.

TODAY'S PLAN

Is there an area of your life where bitterness might be taking root and affecting those around you?

OPPORTUNITIES

TODAY'S PROMISE

We must quickly carry out the tasks assigned us by the one who sent us. The night is coming, and then no one can work.

—JOHN 9:4

TODAY'S THOUGHT

God regularly places divine appointments right in front of you—opportunities to do good, help someone in need, or share what you know about God. When you believe that God is presenting you with an opportunity, respond quickly, and be willing to change your plans in order to be fully committed to what God has put before you.

TODAY'S PLAN

How can you be more sensitive to the opportunities God puts in front of you?

APPEARANCE

TODAY'S PROMISE

Charm is deceptive, and beauty does not last; but a woman who fears the LORD will be greatly praised.

—PROVERBS 31:30

TODAY'S THOUGHT

Appearance does matter; just make sure you're looking at the right things. Your body, face, and clothes are only your outward shell, which is constantly in a state of aging and decay. Your soul and character are your inner being, which is ageless and eternal and communicates who you really are. Walking with God causes you to reflect his beauty. There's nothing wrong with paying attention to your physical appearance, but not to the neglect of your spiritual appearance.

TODAY'S PLAN

What kind of beauty are you most trying to convey to others?

FUTURE

TODAY'S PROMISE

"No eye has seen, no ear has heard, and no mind has imagined what God has prepared for those who love him." But it was to us that God revealed these things by his Spirit. For his Spirit searches out everything and shows us God's deep secrets.

—1 CORINTHIANS 2:9-10

TODAY'S THOUGHT

God promises to reveal enough of the future to give you hope. He tells you that there is a heaven, he tells you how to get there, and he tells you that heaven will be more wonderful than you can imagine. To know any more than that would be beyond what anyone could take in. God wants your trust in him to demonstrate your belief that what he promises will happen. Then your faith will be an inspiration and example to others.

TODAY'S PLAN

Where do you need to trust God more concerning your future?

CONTENTMENT

TODAY'S PROMISE

*Don't love money; be satisfied with what you have.
For God has said, "I will never fail you. I will
never abandon you."* —HEBREWS 13:5

> *We brought nothing with us when we came into
> the world, and we can't take anything with us
> when we leave it.* —1 TIMOTHY 6:7

TODAY'S THOUGHT

Contentment is a result of being willing to give
up everything for God. He may not call you to
do that, but he does call you to be willing. Only
then are you truly free to relax in the peace and
security God offers. Contentment isn't found
in how much you have but in what you do for
God with what you do have.

TODAY'S PLAN

Are there things you are not willing to give up for God?

FEAR

TODAY'S PROMISE

God is our refuge and strength, always ready to help in times of trouble. So we will not fear when earthquakes come and the mountains crumble into the sea. —PSALM 46:1-2

TODAY'S THOUGHT

God is greater than the most severe threats you face. You will not be surprised or overcome by trouble if you recognize how sin has corrupted this world and if you ask God to keep you close to his side. He promises to comfort you and assure you that he is with you in any circumstance. He is always ready to help you when you ask.

TODAY'S PLAN

When you are overcome with fear, what can you do to draw closer to God?

OPPRESSION

TODAY'S PROMISE

[The Lord] has sent me to proclaim that captives will be released, that the blind will see, that the oppressed will be set free, and that the time of the LORD's favor has come.
—LUKE 4:18-19

TODAY'S THOUGHT

Jesus came to deliver people who were oppressed by the world and the powers of evil. We see this in the gospels when he delivered people from demonic oppression. He delivered them from physical oppression by healing their diseases. He delivered them from intellectual oppression by exposing lies and teaching the truth that set them free. Jesus promises to deliver you from those forces that oppress you in this world.

TODAY'S PLAN

Do you need to be delivered from some form of oppression? Have you asked Jesus to set you free?

DECISIONS

TODAY'S PROMISE

Oh, that we might know the LORD! Let us press on to know him. He will respond to us as surely as the arrival of dawn or the coming of rains in early spring.

—HOSEA 6:3

TODAY'S THOUGHT

Sometimes the right decision is simply being faithful in little things. Regular obedience to God brings a regular response from God in guidance and blessing. God's will for you today is that you obey him, read his Word, serve others, and do what is right. When you have been faithful in this way over time, it sometimes feels as if God is letting you choose which way to go. What is really happening is that you are close enough to God to recognize and agree with his leading in your life.

TODAY'S PLAN

What will help you to be faithful in the little things today?

PERSEVERANCE

TODAY'S PROMISE

God has not given us a spirit of fear and timidity, but of power, love, and self-discipline. —2 TIMOTHY 1:7

TODAY'S THOUGHT

Trials, troubles, and the testing of your faith can either strengthen your resolve or break you down. If you see your problems as stepping stones to greater maturity, you can move ahead with anticipation for what you will become—a person of strong character who can handle any obstacle. If you see your problems as barriers, you will become discouraged, give up, turn back, and never allow yourself to become more than you are right now.

TODAY'S PLAN

When you face problems, do you need an attitude adjustment?

EXPECTATIONS

TODAY'S PROMISE

"My thoughts are nothing like your thoughts," says the LORD. "And my ways are far beyond anything you could imagine."
—ISAIAH 55:8

TODAY'S THOUGHT

Sometimes it seems as if God places unrealistic expectations on us. How can we possibly obey all that he commands? How can we love according to his standards? God understands that humanly speaking these expectations are impossible, but with his help, they become possible. God's greatest expectation is not that you live a perfect life but that you love him with all your heart. When you understand that God doesn't expect you to be perfect, but rather is pleased when you sincerely try to follow him, it becomes a holy moment, because you no longer see him as a strict taskmaster but as a loving encourager.

TODAY'S PLAN

What faulty expectations have you developed about God?

POWER

TODAY'S PROMISE

[Jesus] rebuked the wind and the raging waves. The storm stopped and all was calm! —LUKE 8:24

TODAY'S THOUGHT

The same God who can instantly calm the storm on the Sea of Galilee has the power to calm the storms in your heart, dry up a flood of fear, quench the lust for sin, and control the whirl-wind of life. Whether you have had a dramatic life change or a quiet steady walk of faith, your life can be a living demonstration of God's powerful work within you.

TODAY'S PLAN

What could you tell others about the power of God at work in your life?

CHANGE

TODAY'S PROMISE

Jesus Christ is the same yesterday, today, and forever.
                                    —HEBREWS 13:8

TODAY'S THOUGHT

Change is one of the great constants of life. Some changes are positive: a new friend, a new house, a financial windfall; while others are negative: a tragic loss, a job layoff, a natural disaster. Either way, change can be stressful. The Bible offers two great promises about change: First, God never changes. Second, God calls for an inner change of heart, called *repentance,* that produces an outward change of life, called *obedience.* When God changes your heart, your life will also change for the best.

TODAY'S PLAN

How are you changing in order to be more like your changeless and dependable God?

MISTAKES

TODAY'S PROMISE

If we confess our sins to him, he is faithful and just to forgive us our sins and to cleanse us from all wickedness.

—1 JOHN 1:9

TODAY'S THOUGHT

You may feel your mistakes are too great or too numerous for God to forgive, but his forgiveness is not dependent on whether you deserve it or not. It is not dependent on the size or number of your sins. God wants to forgive you as much as you need his forgiveness. You need only to ask. Then focus forward! The door of the future is too small for the baggage of your past to fit through. Let it go, and walk through the door into a new beginning.

TODAY'S PLAN

What is keeping you in the past? Ask for God's forgiveness. What is one thing you can do to move on today?

ABSENCE

TODAY'S PROMISE

*Be sure of this: I am with you always, even to the
end of the age.* —MATTHEW 28:20

TODAY'S THOUGHT

Sometimes, the greater your troubles are, the farther away God seems. In your darkest hour, you
may feel that God has left you. In a time like this,
don't trust your feelings; trust God's promise that he will never leave you. Rely on what
the Bible tells you is true, not on what you are
feeling.

TODAY'S PLAN

*Does God sometimes seem absent? What can you do to trust that
he is there?*

PURPOSE

TODAY'S PROMISE

If you try to hang on to your life, you will lose it. But if you give up your life for my sake, you will save it.

—MATTHEW 16:25

TODAY'S THOUGHT

Many people think God's grace has "strings attached" because you are called to serve God when you are saved. But service is not just something God wants *from* you. It is something God wants *for* you. There is no greater honor than joining God is his great mission of changing the world for good and helping others see how to have a relationship with him for all eternity.

TODAY'S PLAN

Have you made yourself available to God?

NOURISHMENT

TODAY'S PROMISE

Oh, the joys of those who do not follow the advice of the wicked, or stand around with sinners, or join in with mockers. But they delight in the law of the LORD, meditating on it day and night. They are like trees planted along the riverbank, bearing fruit each season. Their leaves never wither, and they prosper in all they do. —PSALM 1:1-3

TODAY'S THOUGHT

Trees planted along a riverbank receive constant nourishment from the life-giving water that is always being absorbed into the nearby ground. When you avoid the advice and temptations of those who love sin, and place yourself by the spiritual nourishment of God's Word, you will absorb the wisdom and blessings of God. You will mature and produce goodness as God's Word feeds you day by day.

TODAY'S PLAN

Where can you grow so that you will receive the most spiritual nourishment from God?

REFLECTIONS

TODAY'S PROMISE

All of us who have had that veil removed can see and reflect the glory of the Lord. And the Lord—who is the Spirit—makes us more and more like him as we are changed into his glorious image.

—2 CORINTHIANS 3:18

TODAY'S THOUGHT

The longer we live with people, the more we become like them. We adopt certain figures of speech or accents like theirs. We sometimes begin to dress alike, or even think the way they do. The same is true when we live with Christ in us. Our speech gradually becomes gentle and kind, our faces mirror his joy, our attitudes and motives become more pure, and our actions are more service oriented. Can others tell that Christ lives in you?

TODAY'S PLAN

Would your friends say that you are becoming more like Jesus each day or less like him?

INJUSTICE

TODAY'S PROMISE

The righteous LORD loves justice. The virtuous will see his face.

—PSALM 11:7

TODAY'S THOUGHT

You cannot ignore those being treated unjustly. If you do, you are in danger of becoming callous—and even corrupt—when it comes to the needs of others. Allow your heart to move you to be a champion for those who are treated unfairly, and you will become an advocate for those who need your help. God promises that those who work for justice will experience his presence in powerful ways.

TODAY'S PLAN

Are you moved when you see injustice around you?

FAVOR WITH GOD

TODAY'S PROMISE

Joyful are those who listen to me, watching for me daily at my gates, waiting for me outside my home! For whoever finds me finds life and receives favor from the LORD. —PROVERBS 8:34-35

TODAY'S THOUGHT

This verse is talking about wisdom from God. When you make it a daily habit to pursue his wisdom, when you ask for his wisdom inside and outside your home, you will have more joy, because no one can give you better advice and guidance than God can. And no one else knows you better or wants you to succeed more. What greater favor from God could there be than his personal advice on how to live?

TODAY'S PLAN

Are you experiencing the favor of God through the wisdom of God?

PRACTICE

TODAY'S PROMISE

Keep putting into practice all you learned and received from me—everything you heard from me and saw me doing. Then the God of peace will be with you.

—PHILIPPIANS 4:9

TODAY'S THOUGHT

When you are learning to play the piano, you need to start with the basics and practice them over and over. Eventually you master the basics, and only then are you prepared to practice pieces of greater difficulty. Practicing spiritual discipline is just as important for mastering the basics of Christian living and deepening your understanding of God and his call on your life. The more you practice disciplines such as prayer, Bible study, and service, the more you grow in spiritual maturity as you strive to be the person God created you to be.

TODAY'S PLAN

What spiritual disciplines are you practicing?

COURAGE

TODAY'S PROMISE

Don't be afraid, for I am with you. Don't be discouraged, for I am your God. I will strengthen you and help you. I will hold you up with my victorious right hand. —ISAIAH 41:10

TODAY'S THOUGHT

Courage comes from the conviction that you can overcome. Much of this conviction that God will help you comes from reading and studying his Word, where you discover his desire and power to accomplish great things through you. If you are convinced that God will help you overcome the obstacles of life, you will be more courageous in moving ahead.

TODAY'S PLAN

Do you really trust that God will help you face life's challenges? How does trusting this promise give you courage to face the challenges of today?

ENCOURAGEMENT

TODAY'S PROMISE

Let everything you say be good and helpful, so that your words will be an encouragement to those who hear them.
                                        —EPHESIANS 4:29

TODAY'S THOUGHT

It's really true—what you spend most of your time thinking about is what you end up doing. When you're tempted to complain, train yourself instead to be grateful. When you're tempted to gossip about someone, think about that person's good qualities and be complimentary instead. Then your words will always be an encouragement to those around you.

TODAY'S PLAN

Are you known as an encourager?

HEAVEN

TODAY'S PROMISE

You must remain faithful to what you have been taught from the beginning. If you do, you will remain in fellowship with the Son and with the Father. And in this fellowship we enjoy the eternal life he promised us.   —1 JOHN 2:24-25

TODAY'S THOUGHT

At its best, this life always leaves us dissatisfied. Experiences don't usually live up to expectations. Dreams go unfulfilled, and we long for so much more. These longings confirm that our souls are anticipating something beyond what this life can deliver. Heaven is more than cosmic geography. The essence of heaven is a relationship with the God who has promised only the best for you and will spend an eternity delivering on that promise.

TODAY'S PLAN

What are you longing for that has never been fulfilled? Might this be your soul anticipating the great blessings of heaven?

BELIEF

TODAY'S PROMISE

Anyone who believes in God's Son has eternal life.

—JOHN 3:36

TODAY'S THOUGHT

Believing in Jesus gives you hope—for today, tomorrow, and eternity. You have hope for today because God's forgiveness transforms relationships. You have hope for tomorrow because he promises to work in your life to make you all he created you to be. You have hope for eternity because he promises that you will live forever in heaven, where life will be perfectly healthy, meaningful, peaceful, and fulfilling. When the world seems to be a crazy, mixed-up place, believers can be absolutely confident that one day Jesus will make everything right again.

TODAY'S PLAN

Where could you use more hope for today, tomorrow, and the future?

LIMITATIONS

TODAY'S PROMISE

My health may fail, and my spirit may grow weak, but God remains the strength of my heart; he is mine forever.
　　　　　　　　　　　　　　　　　　—PSALM 73:26

TODAY'S THOUGHT

In God's unlimited knowledge he created you with limitations, not to discourage you but to help you realize your need for him. When you accomplish something great despite your limitations, it is obvious that God was working through you and that he deserves the credit. Jesus says that what is humanly impossible is possible with God. The next time life makes you aware of your limitations, see it as an opportunity for God's power to defy your limitations, and enjoy the divine moment of having him work through you to accomplish more than you ever could have dreamed.

TODAY'S PLAN

What limitations most frustrate you? Can you let God work his power through you at those points?

DEPRESSION

TODAY'S PROMISE

[Jesus said,] "I have told you all this so that you may have peace in me. Here on earth you will have many trials and sorrows. But take heart, because I have overcome the world." —JOHN 16:33

Even in darkness I cannot hide from you. To you the night shines as bright as day. Darkness and light are the same to you. —PSALM 139:12

TODAY'S THOUGHT

Jesus understands what it feels like to have your soul crushed to the point of death. When you feel like this, you feel hopeless. But the darkness of depression doesn't have to block out the light of God's healing. Cry out to God even from your darkness. He will hear and hold you close.

TODAY'S PLAN

How can you focus on God's words of encouragement today?

HOLINESS

TODAY'S PROMISE

I, the LORD, am holy, and I make you holy.

—LEVITICUS 21:8

TODAY'S THOUGHT

The word *holy* comes from a word that means "to be separate," "to be set apart." The idea of holiness includes not only moral integrity but also your outlook on life as you realize that you are in the world, but not of it. God promises to help you break free from the attractions of this world so that you can live for him.

TODAY'S PLAN

Do you have a "holy" outlook on life?

CONFUSION

TODAY'S PROMISE

Let us hold tightly without wavering to the hope we affirm, for God can be trusted to keep his promise.

—HEBREWS 10:23

TODAY'S THOUGHT

Confusion comes when you waver, when you are uncertain of which road to take. You will always be confused if you don't even know what you are looking for at the end of the road. But with God's Word as your compass, you can at least be certain about which roads *not* to take. That's a great place to start reducing the confusion in your life.

TODAY'S PLAN

How can you use God's Word to guide you when you are confused?

RESURRECTION

TODAY'S PROMISE

[Jesus said,] "I am the resurrection and the life. Anyone who believes in me will live, even after dying."

—JOHN 11:25

TODAY'S THOUGHT

Jesus' resurrection is one of the keys to the Christian faith. Why? Because just as Jesus promised, he rose from the dead. You can be certain of your own resurrection because Jesus has power over death. And you can be confident that he will keep all of his other promises because he proved himself to be more than just a human leader. He is the Son of God who gives eternal life to all who believe in him.

TODAY'S PLAN

How should Jesus' resurrection affect your perspective on this life?

APRIL

WORDS

TODAY'S PROMISE

If you claim to be religious but don't control your tongue, you are fooling yourself, and your religion is worthless.
                                                    —JAMES 1:26

TODAY'S THOUGHT

God promises that your words show what kind of person you really are. They reveal what's in your heart. You cannot live according to a double standard, speaking one way in church and another way at home, on the job, or with your friends. If you do, you are just fooling yourself about your commitment to following God with all your heart.

TODAY'S PLAN

Are your words pleasing to God wherever you are and whoever you talk to?

CONFESSION

TODAY'S PROMISE

Repent of your sins and turn to God, so that your sins may be wiped away.

—ACTS 3:19

TODAY'S THOUGHT

Confession, which is honestly and humbly acknowledging your sins—the ones you know about and the ones you are unaware of—to God, is one of the first steps in repentance. Confession restores your relationship with God and renews your strength and spirit. When you repent (that is, turn from your sinful way of living and turn to God), God removes your guilt, heals your broken soul, and restores your joy. A heart that truly longs for change is willing to confess sin and is ready for the renewal that only God's forgiveness can bring.

TODAY'S PLAN

In what areas could confession bring renewal in your life?

HOPE

TODAY'S PROMISE

When doubts filled my mind, your comfort gave me renewed hope and cheer. —PSALM 94:19

TODAY'S THOUGHT

Hope is expecting something that has not yet occurred. Faith and patience keep hope alive. Have faith that God will do what he has promised, and be patient while he does it in his own way and time.

TODAY'S PLAN

In what area do you need more hope in God?

FREE GIFT

TODAY'S PROMISE

God saved you by his grace when you believed. And you can't take credit for this; it is a gift from God.

—EPHESIANS 2:8

TODAY'S THOUGHT

It seems too easy. The greatest gift God could ever offer—eternal life in a perfect world—is absolutely free. You just have to accept it by (1) agreeing with God that you sin, (2) acknowledging that your sin cuts you off from God, (3) asking Jesus to forgive your sins, (4) and believing that Jesus is Lord over everything and that he is the Son of God. The gift is yours for the asking.

TODAY'S PLAN

Have you accepted God's gift?

ACCEPTANCE

TODAY'S PROMISE

The Son of God . . . loved me and gave himself for me.
                                                —GALATIANS 2:20

TODAY'S THOUGHT

Your value is not determined by the opinions of others. You are a unique creation of God, and you are redeemed through the death and resurrection of God's Son, Jesus. This divine assessment of your worth is true, regardless of how people treat you.

TODAY'S PLAN

How can you see your value the way God sees it?

ETERNAL LIFE

TODAY'S PROMISE

Jesus [said,] "I am the resurrection and the life. Anyone who believes in me will live, even after dying. Everyone who lives in me and believes in me will never ever die." —JOHN 11:25-26

TODAY'S THOUGHT

Why are we afraid to die? Why do we try so hard to keep living? Because we are uncertain of what happens after we die. On this side of death, we at least know the rules about how things work, even if we don't like them. To die physically is to leave our earthly body and our place in the earthly community. To die spiritually, eternally, is to miss eternal residence in heaven with God and his people and to be separated from God forever. When we die physically, we become even more alive as we take up our residence in heaven. For those who belong to Jesus, death is not the end but only the beginning of an eternity of unspeakable joy with the Lord and with other believers.

TODAY'S PLAN

Do you see death as more of an end than a beginning?

GLORY

TODAY'S PROMISE

I heard a loud shout from the throne, saying, "Look, God's home is now among his people! He will live with them, and they will be his people. God himself will be with them. He will wipe every tear from their eyes, and there will be no more death or sorrow or crying or pain. All these things are gone forever."
—REVELATION 21:3-4

TODAY'S THOUGHT

The promise of Scripture is that God will remove all the sin and struggles of this fallen world and create a new heaven and new earth. The best this world has to offer can't begin to compare with the glory to come!

TODAY'S PLAN

Have you stopped to consider how glorious God's new earth will be?

RESURRECTION

*The angel spoke to the women. "Don't be afraid!"
he said. "I know you are looking for Jesus, who was
crucified. He isn't here! He is risen from the dead,
just as he said would happen."* —MATTHEW 28:5-6

Without the resurrection of Jesus from the
dead, there would be no Christian faith. The
Resurrection is central because it demonstrates
God's power over death and assures you that you
will also be resurrected. The power of God that
brought Jesus back from the dead will also bring
you back to life. Jesus' death was not the end. His
resurrection is the beginning of eternal life for all
who believe in him.

Do you believe?

HEAVEN

TODAY'S PROMISE

We are looking forward to the new heavens and new earth he has promised, a world filled with God's righteousness.

—2 PETER 3:13

TODAY'S THOUGHT

God originally created earth to be heaven—the place where he lived with humankind and walked and talked with people. Although sin changed all that when it separated us from God and corrupted the earth, God originally thought of heavenly paradise as a physical place, with trees and plants, mountains and waterfalls, fruits and vegetables. The Bible refers to the new heaven— the place where we will be reunited with God—as the new earth. If God said the original earth he created was "very good," then the new earth he is preparing for us will be similar and familiar to us.

TODAY'S PLAN

What are some of the misconceptions you might have about heaven?

FUTURE

TODAY'S PROMISE

When the Great Shepherd appears, you will receive a crown of never-ending glory and honor. . . . In his kindness God called you to share in his eternal glory by means of Christ Jesus. So after you have suffered a little while, he will restore, support, and strengthen you, and he will place you on a firm foundation.

—1 PETER 5:4, 10

TODAY'S THOUGHT

As a heaven-bound follower of Jesus, you need to put heaven and earth in perspective. Here, we generally live for a hundred years or less. In heaven, one hundred million years are just the beginning. Since you will spend most of your time in heaven, you need to spend your short time here preparing to live there. This eternal perspective helps you live here on earth with the right priorities, for this life is really only your preparation for life in heaven.

TODAY'S PLAN

What are you doing to prepare for heaven?

GOODNESS

TODAY'S PROMISE

You are controlled by the Spirit if you have the Spirit of God living in you. —ROMANS 8:9

[You] will speak the truth in love, growing in every way more and more like Christ, who is the head of his body, the church. —EPHESIANS 4:15

TODAY'S THOUGHT

To be controlled by the Holy Spirit is to do good things, motivated by love for God and for others. True goodness runs deeper than nice actions; it reflects a heart of integrity. If you want to be a good person, God has to change you from the inside out. As you become more and more like Jesus, your actions will reflect his goodness.

TODAY'S PLAN

Are your good deeds motivated by the right source?

ENEMIES

TODAY'S PROMISE

[Jesus said,] "You have heard the law that says, 'Love your neighbor' and hate your enemy. But I say, love your enemies! Pray for those who persecute you!"

—MATTHEW 5:43-44

TODAY'S THOUGHT

Showing love to one's enemies is always unreasonable—unless you realize that you were once an enemy of God until he forgave you. When you love an enemy, you see him or her as Christ does—a person in need of grace. Getting to that point takes prayer. When you pray for others, you can't help but feel compassion for them. This is how you can have the strength to refrain from retaliating when they hurt you, and this is how God can turn an enemy into a friend.

TODAY'S PLAN

What does it mean to really love your enemies?

HOPE

TODAY'S PROMISE

*Through Christ you have come to trust in God.
And you have placed your faith and hope in God
because he raised Christ from the dead and gave him
  great glory.*
                                                —1 PETER 1:21

TODAY'S THOUGHT

The Lord is our source of hope because his
promises are true. We lose hope when we stop
believing that. The Resurrection, the greatest event in history, is the foundation of your
hope. Jesus promised that he would rise from
the dead, and because he did, you can be assured
that every other promise God makes to you will
also come true.

TODAY'S PLAN

*Do you believe that Jesus died and rose from the dead?
How should this change everything else you believe
about him?*

FAILURE

TODAY'S PROMISE

I cried out, "I am slipping!" but your unfailing love, O LORD, supported me. —PSALM 94:18

TODAY'S THOUGHT

Even heroes of the Bible such as Abraham, Moses, David, and Peter had firsthand experiences with failure. Jesus was the only man on earth who ever led a truly perfect life, but he was God! Fortunately, failure is not fatal. It does not mean you are substandard—only human. What you learn from your failure is what really counts. No matter how many times you fail, you can trust God to help pick you up, love you, and encourage you to move forward.

TODAY'S PLAN

Do you ever feel as if everyone else has the perfect life and you're the one who fails? Then remember that it is in your failures that God is most ready to pick you up with his supporting arms.

JESUS

TODAY'S PROMISE

All of God's promises have been fulfilled in Christ with a resounding "Yes!" And through Christ, our "Amen" (which means "Yes") ascends to God for his glory.
—2 CORINTHIANS 1:20

TODAY'S THOUGHT

Jesus Christ is the Messiah who was promised by God. He was fully God and fully human. He lived a sinless life so that he could die on the cross to take the punishment that you deserve for your sins. Then he rose from the dead, proving that he has power even over death. If you believe in him as Lord, you also will be raised to eternal life. Those who believe in Jesus have the promise of living forever in heaven with him.

TODAY'S PLAN

Do you believe God's promises about Jesus? If not, what would it take for you to believe?

FAITH

TODAY'S PROMISE

Faith is the confidence that what we hope for will actually happen; it gives us assurance about things we cannot see. —HEBREWS 11:1

TODAY'S THOUGHT

Faith gives you hope. When the world seems to be a crazy, mixed-up place, believers can be absolutely confident that one day Jesus will come and make it right again. Your faith in his promise to do that someday will enable you to keep going today.

TODAY'S PLAN

How is your faith giving you hope?

CHALLENGES

TODAY'S PROMISE

Be strong and courageous, and do the work. Don't be afraid or discouraged, for the LORD God, my God, is with you. He will not fail you or forsake you. He will see to it that all the work . . . is finished correctly.

—1 CHRONICLES 28:20

TODAY'S THOUGHT

Regardless of the size of the task, God's strength working in you is sufficient to help you see any task through to completion. God will never call you to a task without going with you to see it through. He will provide all that you need.

TODAY'S PLAN

If you've been called to a difficult task, how will it help you to know that God will provide all you need to accomplish what is necessary today?

NEW BODIES

It is the same way with the resurrection of the dead. Our earthly bodies are planted in the ground when we die, but they will be raised to live forever.

—1 CORINTHIANS 15:42

Your body will get sick and become a burden to you. It will age and deteriorate. You really wouldn't want to live in it forever. Think how many physical problems you would accumulate over a few thousand years! The Bible teaches that in heaven God will give you a new physical body that will never age or deteriorate, get sick, or become disabled. Your new body will be perfect and beautiful, and you will never be ashamed of it again.

Picture what it will be like to have a perfect body that will never age or sin.

GRACE

TODAY'S PROMISE

[God] has reconciled you to himself through the death of Christ in his physical body. As a result, he has brought you into his own presence, and you are holy and blameless as you stand before him without a single fault.

—COLOSSIANS 1:22

TODAY'S THOUGHT

Without the grace of God, your faults would cause you to live under the burden of constant guilt because you can never measure up to God's standards. You can never obey him enough. Yet Jesus' sacrifice on the cross frees you to live in a wonderful relationship with God. His grace forgets your faults so that he actually looks at you as though you have never sinned! This should motivate you to live faultless before him, not out of guilt but out of love.

TODAY'S PLAN

Do you live under guilt or under grace?

ENDURANCE

TODAY'S PROMISE

Patient endurance is what you need now, so that you will continue to do God's will. Then you will receive all that he has promised. —HEBREWS 10:36

TODAY'S THOUGHT

Endurance is an essential quality for Jesus' followers. It is the only way to complete God's purpose for you. Though you have the promise of eternal life, you also face the prospect of living in a fallen world that is out to compromise and destroy your faith. God promises that those who endure in their faith will not only survive but will also live with him forever!

TODAY'S PLAN

In what areas of your life do you need more endurance? How can your future hope help you to endure today?

DOUBT

TODAY'S PROMISE

Let's not get tired of doing what is good. At just the right time we will reap a harvest of blessing if we don't give up.
　　　　　　　　　　　　　　　　—GALATIANS 6:9

TODAY'S THOUGHT

When troubles come your way and you begin to doubt that what you believe is really true, you need to continue to be obedient. What makes doubt spiritually healthy or unhealthy is what you do with it. You can allow it to debilitate your faith, or you can let it carry you right back to God. Bring your questions, as well as your doubts, to him, and he will restore your faith.

TODAY'S PLAN

In what area are you getting tired of doing good? This is where doubt will attack you.

COURAGE

TODAY'S PROMISE

Having hope will give you courage. —JOB 11:18

TODAY'S THOUGHT

Without hope there is no courage. The courage to face trouble and danger comes when you have hope for a better future on the other side of adversity. Courage does not always mean fearlessness. You can be afraid and still have hope. Courage is walking in faith in spite of your fear and trusting God's promise that your eternal future is secure. Never lose hope, and you will find the courage to meet the challenges ahead of you.

TODAY'S PLAN

What do you hope for? Does this hope chase away your fears or produce other fears? If you find yourself lacking the courage to face your troubles, check to see who or what you're hoping in.

LOYALTY

TODAY'S PROMISE

I no longer call you slaves, because a master doesn't confide in his slaves. Now you are my friends, since I have told you everything the Father told me.

—JOHN 15:15

TODAY'S THOUGHT

Think of the qualities you look for in a friend. Perhaps you would list honesty, loyalty, or availability. God desires these same qualities from you as his friend. He wants you to come to him with honesty about your struggles and successes, to remain faithful and loyal to him and his Word, and to make yourself available to spend quality time with him. You fear separation in your own friendships—how much more should you fear separation from God? Respect him, honor him, and remain loyal to him; he will call you a friend.

TODAY'S PLAN

Would God call you a loyal friend?

ETERNITY

TODAY'S PROMISE

God has made everything beautiful for its own time. He has planted eternity in the human heart, but even so, people cannot see the whole scope of God's work from beginning to end. —ECCLESIASTES 3:11

TODAY'S THOUGHT

Because you are created in God's image, you have eternal value, and nothing but the eternal God can satisfy your deepest longings. He has built into you a restless yearning for the kind of perfect world that can be found only in heaven. Someday he will restore earth to the way it was when he first created it, when it was perfect, and eternity will be a never ending exploration of its beauty and a perfect relationship with God.

TODAY'S PLAN

How should your hope of eternal life affect the way you live now?

PROTECTION

TODAY'S PROMISE

[The Lord's] faithful promises are your armor and protection. Do not be afraid of the terrors of the night, nor the arrow that flies in the day. . . . For he will order his angels to protect you wherever you go.

—PSALM 91:4-5, 11

TODAY'S THOUGHT

This passage of Scripture has been a constant source of courage and encouragement throughout the centuries. It reminds you that although the threats in this world seem endless, the promise of God's eternal protection is infinitely greater. Sooner or later your earthly body will die, but God promises never to let evil conquer and enslave his followers for eternity.

TODAY'S PLAN

How does knowing that God has victory over evil help you to live courageously now?

TRANSFORMING POWER

TODAY'S PROMISE

The Holy Spirit produces this kind of fruit in our lives: love, joy, peace, patience, kindness, goodness, faithfulness, gentleness, and self-control.

—GALATIANS 5:22-23

TODAY'S THOUGHT

When you invite God into your life, you are also asking him to use his power to change you. He won't force change on you, but if you ask, you have the power of God himself to begin a work of transformation that lasts a lifetime. Your character and choices will mature, and others will see the fruit of God's transforming power growing in you.

TODAY'S PLAN

Can you find the courage to ask God to unleash his transforming power in you?

WORSHIP

This is what the LORD says: "Heaven is my throne, and the earth is my footstool. Could you build me a temple as good as that? Could you build me such a resting place? My hands have made both heaven and earth; they and everything in them are mine. I, the LORD, have spoken! I will bless those who have humble and contrite hearts, who tremble at my word." —ISAIAH 66:1-2

TODAY'S THOUGHT

To worship is to ascribe ultimate value to an object, a person, or God—and then to revere, adore, pay homage to, and obey by ordering the priorities of your life around what you worship. God alone is worthy of your worship. And worship, more than anything else, will connect you with God, your only source of lasting hope.

TODAY'S PLAN

What do your priorities say about what or whom you worship?

PEACE OF MIND

TODAY'S PROMISE

[Jesus said,] "I am leaving you with a gift—peace of mind and heart. And the peace I give is a gift the world cannot give. So don't be troubled or afraid."

—JOHN 14:27

TODAY'S THOUGHT

Jesus didn't leave this world to abandon you to face your fears and troubles alone. He left so that he could give to the world the gift of the Holy Spirit to be with all believers at all times. The Spirit within you is a gift from God that provides peace of mind and heart in the face of your greatest fears.

TODAY'S PLAN

Do you realize that peace of mind comes from the Holy Spirit who lives within you?

BROKENNESS

TODAY'S PROMISE

The sacrifice you desire is a broken spirit. You will not reject a broken and repentant heart, O God.

—PSALM 51:17

TODAY'S THOUGHT

When you sin, you must fall to your knees to be restored to God. When you're confronted by your failure or sin, don't run from God. Don't make excuses or give up in despair. Instead, acknowledge your need for God's help. He promises to draw close to you when you are broken about the sin in your life and to begin the process of healing and restoration.

TODAY'S PLAN

Where do you need healing and restoration in your relationship with God or others?

ENCOURAGEMENT

[God] has enabled you to share in the inheritance that belongs to his people, who live in the light. For he has rescued us from the kingdom of darkness and transferred us into the Kingdom of his dear Son, who purchased our freedom and forgave our sins.

—COLOSSIANS 1:12-14

TODAY'S THOUGHT

Be encouraged that you have been rescued from sin's control and Satan's power. God, through the power of his Holy Spirit, has given you all you need to overcome whatever overwhelms you. When you remember that you are already free from sin's deadly power, the problems of this world lose much of their grip on you.

TODAY'S PLAN

Does knowing that you are no longer under sin's control encourage you to live more faithfully for God?

MAY

NEIGHBORS

TODAY'S PROMISE

Indeed, it is good when you obey the royal law as found in the Scriptures: "Love your neighbor as yourself."

—JAMES 2:8

TODAY'S THOUGHT

A neighbor is not merely someone who happens to live near you and be like you. A neighbor is anyone who has a need you can meet. To love your neighbor is to choose to meet that need, regardless of how different the person is or how inconvenient helping him or her turns out to be.

TODAY'S PLAN

Who are the neighbors in your life right now? What can you do to help them?

BIBLE

TODAY'S PROMISE

All Scripture is inspired by God and is useful to teach us what is true and to make us realize what is wrong in our lives. It corrects us when we are wrong and teaches us to do what is right. God uses it to prepare and equip his people to do every good work.

—2 TIMOTHY 3:16-17

TODAY'S THOUGHT

When you buy a new computer but fail to read the instruction manual, you miss out on all that the machine is capable of doing. You're operating with just enough knowledge to do basic functions. When it comes to reading the Bible, most of us read just enough to get by. We miss much that God's Word has to offer. Read the Bible daily so that you can thoroughly understand all God wants you to know, and then you will be equipped to live at peak performance.

TODAY'S PLAN

What can you do to develop a more regular habit of reading God's Word?

GUIDANCE

TODAY'S PROMISE

The LORD directs the steps of the godly. He delights in every detail of their lives. —PSALM 37:23

TODAY'S THOUGHT

When you are anxious or concerned, often what you most often need is the assurance that God does care about you and is watching over you. If God values the little details of his creation, how much more must he value the details and direction of your life.

TODAY'S PLAN

Do you bother God with the details of your life? He wants you to.

HOLY SPIRIT

TODAY'S PROMISE

I pray that from his glorious, unlimited resources he will empower you with inner strength through his Spirit.

—EPHESIANS 3:16

TODAY'S THOUGHT

The Holy Spirit is the power of God that lives in every believer. When you yield control of your life to the Lord, he releases his power within you—power to resist temptation, to serve and love him and others when you are at the end of your rope, to have wisdom in all circumstances, and to persevere in living for God now with the promise of eternal life later. Through his Spirit, God will give you the energy you need to do all that he asks you to do.

TODAY'S PLAN

Are you relying on God's Holy Spirit to work through you?

CREATIVITY

TODAY'S PROMISE

We are God's masterpiece. He has created us anew in Christ Jesus, so we can do the good things he planned for us long ago. —EPHESIANS 2:10

TODAY'S THOUGHT

God created you to do good things, and to do good things, you must be creative. He built creativity into you for the specific purpose of carrying out the work he wants you to do. God made you creative so that you could express yourself in numerous different ways—in worship, singing, loving, helping, in music, crafting things, and thinking through problems. When the expression of your creativity accomplishes the work God had in mind for you, you become a masterpiece, a beautiful expression of God's image doing God's work for God's people.

TODAY'S PLAN

How are you using your creativity to accomplish what God created you for?

INTEGRITY

TODAY'S PROMISE

I will bring that group through the fire and make them pure. I will refine them like silver and purify them like gold. They will call on my name, and I will answer them. I will say, "These are my people," and they will say, "The LORD is our God."

—ZECHARIAH 13:9

TODAY'S THOUGHT

Just as fire is necessary for refining gold, the heat and pressure of trouble refines your integrity. Every day is a refining process that tests how pure you are becoming. If God finds your heart and actions becoming increasingly pure, then you are living more in union with him and are growing in integrity. Thank God for the ways he is shaping your character, and ask him to prepare you to respond with integrity to the tests ahead.

TODAY'S PLAN

Are your troubles and pressures refining your integrity?

EXAMPLE

TODAY'S PROMISE

[Jesus said,] "No one lights a lamp and then puts it under a basket. Instead, a lamp is placed on a stand, where it gives light to everyone in the house. In the same way, let your good deeds shine out for all to see, so that everyone will praise your heavenly Father." —MATTHEW 5:15-16

TODAY'S THOUGHT

An authentic Christian lifestyle is a witness to the community at large. What people say about the way you live will probably have the greatest impact on what they think about what you believe, and even about other Christians. Your actions will either attract or repel others to your faith.

TODAY'S PLAN

What are others saying about you when you aren't in the room?

OVERWHELMED

TODAY'S PROMISE

Each one of you will put to flight a thousand of the enemy, for the LORD your God fights for you, just as he has promised.

—JOSHUA 23:10

TODAY'S THOUGHT

Be encouraged that the power of God is for you, regardless of the number of enemies against you. God used David to overcome Goliath. He used Gideon's three hundred soldiers to defeat the vast armies of Midian. And he used twelve disciples to establish the world-wide church. Knowing that he enjoys working through your weaknesses and limitations can be a great encouragement. You don't have to be smart or strong or beautiful for God to do great things through you.

TODAY'S PLAN

In what areas of your life do you feel the weakest? What most overwhelms you? Maybe these are the areas where God wants to use you the most!

LOVE

TODAY'S PROMISE

Don't just pretend to love others. Really love them.

—ROMANS 12:9

TODAY'S THOUGHT

It's easy to like people who are likeable, but we model more of God's love when we serve those who are annoying. You'll never find a perfect church, and you'll never find a perfect group of people—even among Christians—so don't go looking for that. Instead, seek God's guidance as to where you should be, and then take joy in reaching out and loving those God has placed in your sphere of influence. You may be surprised at how the power of God can bring the most unlikely people together as friends. When you reach out to others in love, your heart is also changed.

TODAY'S PLAN

Who is annoying you these days? What can you do to show love for that person?

CONFIDENCE

TODAY'S PROMISE

The LORD keeps watch over you as you come and go, both now and forever. —PSALM 121:8

TODAY'S THOUGHT

Many great athletes say their real contest is mental, not physical. It's the same way in your spiritual life. Your confidence comes not from your physical circumstances (how you look or what you achieve), but from that inner assurance that God is by your side, making his wisdom and power available to you daily, and working out his best plan for your life.

TODAY'S PLAN

How confident are you that God is working for you and in you every day?

LISTENING

TODAY'S PROMISE

My children, listen to me, for all who follow my ways are joyful.
—PROVERBS 8:32

TODAY'S THOUGHT

Just as a piano is tuned against a standard tuning fork, so you become in tune with God only when you compare yourself against the standards for living found in the Bible. As God communicates to you through his Word, you will begin to "hear," or discern just what he wants of you. As your "spiritual hearing" is fine tuned, you will become a good listener and will be able to hear clearly when God calls you to a certain task that he has reserved just for you.

TODAY'S PLAN

Would God say you are a good listener?

SPIRIT-CONTROLLED

TODAY'S PROMISE

Let the Holy Spirit guide your lives. Then you won't be doing what your sinful nature craves.

—GALATIANS 5:16

TODAY'S THOUGHT

When your life is controlled by the Holy Spirit of God, you will have far less interest in sinful pleasures. In your own strength, you cannot live a pure or holy life, but with the spirit of God in you, you can make steady progress toward purity and holiness until that day when you meet God face to face in eternity, completely pure and holy.

TODAY'S PLAN

How spirit-controlled are you?

CIRCUMSTANCES

TODAY'S PROMISE

You suffered along with those who were thrown into jail, and when all you owned was taken from you, you accepted it with joy. You knew there were better things waiting for you that will last forever.

—HEBREWS 10:34

TODAY'S THOUGHT

Accepting your circumstances doesn't mean you have to like them. But by keeping an eternal perspective that this life is not all there is, you can learn from and grow through difficult times. Remember that difficult circumstances will not follow you to heaven; one day, you will be in a place where there will be no more tears or sorrow. One day, God will make all things right.

TODAY'S PLAN

Do you have enough faith to see the end of your difficult circumstances?

MAY 14

HEALTH

Physical training is good, but training for godliness is much better, promising benefits in this life and in the life to come. —1 TIMOTHY 4:8

TODAY'S THOUGHT

God cares deeply about the condition of both your body and your soul. Spiritual exercise is as purposeful and strenuous as physical exercise. But it is important to remember that the benefits of physical fitness lasts only as long as your body does. Spiritual fitness lasts for eternity. Knowing the eternally long-term benefits of spiritual exercise should motivate you to keep your physical and spiritual health in a wholesome balance and help you to experience a vibrant relationship with your Creator.

TODAY'S PLAN

Are you getting enough spiritual exercise?

FAITHFULNESS

TODAY'S PROMISE

Don't be afraid. . . . If you remain faithful even when facing death, I will give you the crown of life.

—REVELATION 2:10

TODAY'S THOUGHT

Faithfulness brings rewards—both in this life and for eternity. God is aware of the way you approach life and is pleased when you are loyal to him. Others will also recognize your reputation for faithfulness and loyalty. Faithfulness to God helps you avoid trouble and gain security. The best reason to be faithful, however, is that God promises to be faithful to you when you sincerely try to follow him.

TODAY'S PLAN

How can you be inspired by God's faithfulness to you? In what ways can you remain faithful to him today?

KINDNESS

TODAY'S PROMISE

If you give even a cup of cold water to one of the least of my followers, you will surely be rewarded.

—MATTHEW 10:42

TODAY'S THOUGHT

God rewards kindness because it demonstrates unconditional love, the supreme character trait of a Christian. True kindness is not a single act but a lifestyle. Begin showing kindness in the small things you do and say until you are truly kind in all situations. Kindness is not motivated by reward, but you will be rewarded for your kindness.

TODAY'S PLAN

What small act of kindness can you show to someone today? What can you do to show kindness to someone you don't like, or don't know?

CONTROL

TODAY'S PROMISE

Give all your worries and cares to God, for he cares about you. —1 PETER 5:7

Taste and see that the LORD is good. Oh, the joys of those who take refuge in him! —PSALM 34:8

TODAY'S THOUGHT

Have you ever been late for an appointment because you were stuck in traffic? Has it ever rained every day of a long-awaited vacation? Have you lost a good friend? Sooner or later we all face situations beyond our control. The Bible teaches that even when you find yourself in unpredictable, uncontrollable, and frustrating circumstances, there is one thing you can control: your reaction to the situation. You can trust God to work in your life to bring order, hope, and peace out of chaos.

TODAY'S PLAN

What has gone out of control for you? How can you give it over to God?

AFFECTION

TODAY'S PROMISE

Guard your heart above all else, for it determines the course of your life. —PROVERBS 4:23

TODAY'S THOUGHT

Whatever you regard with high affection will determine the direction of your life. Be sure your highest affections will direct you to life's greatest goal—a relationship with Jesus. Be careful to guard your affections, realizing how improper desires can have a disastrous impact on your life and your family.

TODAY'S PLAN

What should you do if your affection for God is waning, or if some of your affections are misplaced?

EMPTINESS

TODAY'S PROMISE

You know that God paid a ransom to save you from the empty life you inherited from your ancestors.

—1 PETER 1:18

TODAY'S THOUGHT

A heart without God filling it is an empty heart. Don't confuse accomplishment with purpose. You may do a lot and accomplish much, but after a while it all feels empty and meaningless if there is no lasting purpose behind what you do. That is why Jesus came to give you a fulfilling life of purpose and eternal blessings.

TODAY'S PLAN

How much of your heart is filled with God?

PRIORITIES

TODAY'S PROMISE

Wherever your treasure is, there the desires of your heart will also be. —LUKE 12:34

TODAY'S THOUGHT

When God is the center of your life, your relationship with him will be your highest priority. You will long to spend time with him in prayer and reading the Bible, your thoughts will often turn to him, you will want to please him and obey him. The more you love God, the more your heart will long to be closer to his.

TODAY'S PLAN

What do you value most? What do you think about most? That reveals what's in your heart. Is God there?

GIVING

TODAY'S PROMISE

If you give even a cup of cold water to one of the least of my followers, you will surely be rewarded.

—MATTHEW 10:42

TODAY'S THOUGHT

The simplest gifts often bring the most sacred rewards. No gift is too small, and no act of kindness is too insignificant to be unnoticed by God. Even giving the smallest gifts blesses you with the joy of pleasing God and the satisfaction of helping others.

TODAY'S PLAN

What small gift might you give someone today?

BELONGING

TODAY'S PROMISE

The eternal God is your refuge, and his everlasting arms are under you. —DEUTERONOMY 33:27

TODAY'S THOUGHT

We all need a sense of belonging, for in belonging is security and acceptance. When you're feeling isolated or alone, remember that God has accepted you, adopted you, and welcomed you into his own family. You rest in his arms, which will carry you through life and into eternity.

TODAY'S PLAN

Do you feel as if you belong to God?

CRISIS

TODAY'S PROMISE

The LORD says, "I will guide you along the best pathway for your life. I will advise you and watch over you."

—PSALM 32:8

TODAY'S THOUGHT

You need not pray for the Lord to be with you in times of crisis—he is already there. Instead, pray that you will recognize his presence and have the humility and discernment to accept his help.

TODAY'S PLAN

When you face a crisis, do you think God's gone away, or are you expecting to see him at any moment?

MATURITY

TODAY'S PROMISE

Let your roots grow down into him, and let your lives be built on him. Then your faith will grow strong in the truth you were taught, and you will overflow with thankfulness.

—COLOSSIANS 2:7

TODAY'S THOUGHT

Spiritual growth is like physical growth—you start small and grow one day at a time. As you grow, however, you need more nourishment. Spiritually you get this by challenging your mind to study God's Word, ask questions about it, and seek answers through prayer, the counsel of other believers, and life's experiences. Look at each day as a building block, and before you know it, you will be on your way to spiritual maturity.

TODAY'S PLAN

What small step of maturity can you take today?

FULL LIFE

TODAY'S PROMISE

May you experience the love of Christ, though it is too great to understand fully. Then you will be made complete with all the fullness of life and power that comes from God. —EPHESIANS 3:19

TODAY'S THOUGHT

Too often we define abundance quantitatively by how many possessions or how much financial wealth we have. Instead, think of abundance as God does—the marvelous gift of salvation and eternal life; the blessing of a relationship with the Creator of the universe; the treasure of God's Word; and the wonderful character traits of godliness, truth, wisdom, and a good reputation. These riches are lasting and priceless, and this abundance is guaranteed by your obedience and faith in Jesus.

TODAY'S PLAN

How much of the "fullness of life" are you experiencing?

ROMANCE

TODAY'S PROMISE

[God said,] "I will make you my wife forever, showing you righteousness and justice, unfailing love and compassion. I will be faithful to you and make you mine, and you will finally know me as the LORD."

—HOSEA 2:19-20

TODAY'S THOUGHT

As you read through the Bible, you learn that God is a romantic who desires an intimate relationship with you. He desires your constant company, and is interested in the smallest details of your life. As you realize your precious value to God, you will find confidence in your faith, strength to be faithful to him, and a deep hunger and desire to know more of him.

TODAY'S PLAN

Are you captivated by God's love for you?

RENEWAL

TODAY'S PROMISE

That is why we never give up. Though our bodies are dying, our spirits are being renewed every day.

—2 CORINTHIANS 4:16

TODAY'S THOUGHT

How often we disappoint ourselves. We have such high hopes and pure intentions but inevitably, we find ourselves weary and burnt out with self-defeat or the burdens of life. The messiness of life can leave us feeling exhausted not only physically but also spiritually, in our very souls. If only we could start over. So many of us are in desperate need of renewal. Renewal begins with the compassion of God and a heart ready for change. When the two are put together, we find a new beginning, a soul refreshed, and a life revived.

TODAY'S PLAN

In what ways can God renew you?

COMFORT

TODAY'S PROMISE

Even when I walk through the darkest valley, I will not be afraid, for you are close beside me. Your rod and your staff protect and comfort me. —PSALM 23:4

TODAY'S THOUGHT

Intimacy with God provides a close relationship that helps you see his personal touch on your life every day. He is your shepherd and creator. He wants to communicate with you, watch out for you, care for you, advise you, and give you his joy and blessings. Work with him as he guides you, step-by-step. When you stay close to him, you will see him act on your behalf. Look for him in your life today, and you will notice him.

TODAY'S PLAN

In what ways can you draw closer to God to more fully experience his comfort?

SATISFACTION

TODAY'S PROMISE

When I discovered your words, I devoured them. They are my joy and my heart's delight. —JEREMIAH 15:16

The laws of the LORD are true. . . . They are sweeter than honey, even honey dripping from the comb. —PSALM 19:9-10

TODAY'S THOUGHT

When you're hungry, the worst thing you can do is eat the wrong thing. The same principle applies to satisfying the hungry soul. Fill it with only fun, pleasure, or sin and you'll always be craving more and never get enough. Without taking nourishment from God's spiritual food you will never feel truly satisfied.

TODAY'S PLAN

Is your soul craving the right nourishment?

FREEDOM

TODAY'S PROMISE

I urge you, first of all, to pray for all people. Ask God to help them; intercede on their behalf, and give thanks for them. Pray this way for kings and all who are in authority so that we can live peaceful and quiet lives marked by godliness and dignity.

—1 TIMOTHY 2:1-2

TODAY'S THOUGHT

It's important to pray for your nation, for God says this can lead to peace. Pray that it will be protected by God's mighty hand. Pray for your leaders to be humble and wise, able to discern right from wrong, and to be champions of the needy and helpless. A nation that condones and endorses immorality is subject to judgment and will eventually collapse from the inside out. A nation that collectively worships the one true God will stand firm.

TODAY'S PLAN

How can you pray for your country today?

PEACE

TODAY'S PROMISE

Turn away from evil and do good. Search for peace, and work to maintain it. The eyes of the LORD watch over those who do right; his ears are open to their cries for help. —PSALM 34:14-15

TODAY'S THOUGHT

We are called to work and pray for peace in the world. This will happen as more people make peace with God—and truly understand what that means. When you pursue peace with others, God says he is more actively involved in your life. Why? Because people who pursue peace are pursuing his agenda. With God's help and your commitment to peace, you can make a difference.

TODAY'S PLAN

Is peace on your agenda—in your relationships and in the world?

JUNE

NEEDS

TODAY'S PROMISE

God . . . will supply all your needs from his glorious riches, which have been given to us in Christ Jesus.

—PHILIPPIANS 4:19

TODAY'S THOUGHT

You must learn to distinguish between wants and needs. When you understand what you truly need and see how God provides, you will realize how much he truly cares for you. God doesn't promise to give you a lot of possessions, but he does promise to help you possess the character traits that reflect his nature so that you can accomplish his plan for you. He doesn't promise to preserve your physical life, but he does promise to keep your soul for all eternity if you've pledged your allegiance to him.

TODAY'S PLAN

Make a list of your needs and wants. Would God have the same list? What might he change?

DIGNITY

TODAY'S PROMISE

What are people that you should think about them,
mere mortals that you should care for them? Yet
you made them only a little lower than God and
crowned them with glory and honor. You gave
them charge of everything you made, putting
all things under their authority. —PSALM 8:4-6

TODAY'S THOUGHT

Dignity is the fruit of understanding who God
made you to be—a human being who bears his
image. In the eyes of the Creator, you have great
worth and value and have been made for a special
purpose. Your dignity comes not from what others think about you, but from the fact that God
chose to create you with unique spiritual gifts
and abilities. You have great worth in the
eyes of God, and this should give you the
confidence to boldly serve him wherever he
leads you.

TODAY'S PLAN

Do you see yourself as a person of worth in God's eyes?

JUNE 3

HEAVEN

TODAY'S PROMISE

[Jesus said,] "I am the way, the truth, and the life. No one can come to the Father except through me."

—JOHN 14:6

TODAY'S THOUGHT

Jesus is the only way to heaven—that's a promise. You may want to buy your way in, work your way in, think your way in. But the Bible is clear— Jesus Christ provides the only way in. Believing it and gratefully accepting it is the only way to get to life's most important destination.

TODAY'S PLAN

Have you been trying to get into heaven a different way?

CHARACTER

TODAY'S PROMISE

God blesses those whose hearts are pure, for they will see God. —MATTHEW 5:8

TODAY'S THOUGHT

God promises that when you desire to become more like him, your heart will become purer, and your character will reflect his. And the more you reflect God's character, the more you will be able to understand God and see him at work all around you.

TODAY'S PLAN

Is your heart pure enough to see God at work?

BEAUTY

TODAY'S PROMISE

Don't be concerned about the outward beauty of fancy hairstyles, expensive jewelry, or beautiful clothes. You should clothe yourselves instead with the beauty that comes from within, the unfading beauty of a gentle and quiet spirit, which is so precious to God. —1 PETER 3:3-5

TODAY'S THOUGHT

The world focuses on outward beauty, which fades and does not last. The bodies of Christians will one day be transformed and will no longer age or deteriorate. It is good to care for your physical body, but you should also focus on developing your inward beauty. You may not see yourself as physically beautiful, but your godliness will help others see the real beauty in you.

TODAY'S PLAN

Do you working as hard on your inner beauty as on your outward appearance?

HEALING

TODAY'S PROMISE

My grace is all you need. My power works best in weakness. —2 CORINTHIANS 12:9

TODAY'S THOUGHT

We do not know why God heals some people and not others. But we do know that God's power is magnified through our weaknesses and infirmities as he works within us. If you have been praying for healing for yourself or for a loved one and God has not done it, trust that he will do something great in your situation, whether or not physical healing takes place.

TODAY'S PLAN

Where are you weak or hurting? Watch right there for God to work his power through you.

REDEEMING THE BAD

TODAY'S PROMISE

So, my dear brothers and sisters, be strong and immovable. Always work enthusiastically for the Lord, for you know that nothing you do for the Lord is ever useless. —1 CORINTHIANS 15:58

TODAY'S THOUGHT

Believe that God is working in your life to use both the good and the bad for a greater purpose. Nothing that happens to you is a waste. Disappointment turns into hope as you watch God redeem your current adversity, and even your mistakes.

TODAY'S PLAN

What are you doing now that seems fruitless? How might you see God redeeming this time for something good?

GRACE

TODAY'S PROMISE

Sin is no longer your master, for you no longer live under the requirements of the law. Instead, you live under the freedom of God's grace. —ROMANS 6:14

TODAY'S THOUGHT

What you believe about God is the most important conviction you can have, because it determines your whole world view. When you believe the depth of his love and grace toward you, you live with the joy of being forgiven and knowing you will live forever in heaven. You no longer fear God's retribution, but look forward to a relationship with him.

TODAY'S PLAN

How does the way you live reveal what you believe about God? How can you live in a way that reveals God's grace and forgiveness?

BETRAYAL

TODAY'S PROMISE

This High Priest of ours understands our weaknesses.

—HEBREWS 4:15

God has said, "I will never fail you. I will never abandon you."

—HEBREWS 13:5

TODAY'S THOUGHT

There is comfort in the fact that because Jesus was betrayed, he personally understands your pain. He who has the power to help you has experienced your hurt himself. When others are unfaithful to you, take great comfort in God's unwavering faithfulness. He promises never to abandon his relationship with you.

TODAY'S PLAN

Will you make a daily commitment to talk with the One who you can trust the most?

EVIL

TODAY'S PROMISE

I went into your sanctuary, O God, and I finally understood the destiny of the wicked. Truly, you put them on a slippery path and send them sliding over the cliff to destruction. In an instant they are destroyed, completely swept away by terrors.

—PSALM 73:17-20

TODAY'S THOUGHT

Sometimes it seems that evil people can do anything they want and not only get away with it but also prosper. God has promised, however, that in his time everyone will be judged, evil will be exposed, and the righteous will prevail. God doesn't promise the absence of evil on this earth. In fact, he warns that evil will be pervasive and powerful. But God promises to help you stand against evil, and if you do, you will receive your reward in heaven, where evil will be no more.

TODAY'S PLAN

Are you letting God help you stand against evil?

HOLY SPIRIT

TODAY'S PROMISE

He generously poured out the Spirit upon us through Jesus Christ our Savior. —TITUS 3:6

TODAY'S THOUGHT

One of God's most generous gifts is the presence of his Holy Spirit in all who believe in him. God doesn't give this gift only to the ultra-righteous or giants of the faith. He gives his presence to everyone who believes in Jesus as the way to heaven and eternal life. The Holy Spirit encourages you to live for God, keeps your focus on heaven, and protects you from being defeated by the enemy.

TODAY'S PLAN

Are you using God's gift of his Spirit to help you in life's journey?

EXAMPLE

TODAY'S PROMISE

Be careful to live properly among your unbelieving neighbors. Then even if they accuse you of doing wrong, they will see your honorable behavior, and they will give honor to God when he judges the world.
—1 PETER 2:12

TODAY'S THOUGHT

You can be an example to others by treating them with love and respect, living honorably and graciously before them, striving for godliness, and refusing to judge them. If they don't know God, why should you expect them to live as though they do? Instead of being critical, be an example of a life shining with the love of Jesus, and then some of them will be drawn to believe in him as well.

TODAY'S PLAN

Is your godly behavior motivating others to have godly behavior as well?

DIFFERENCE MAKER

TODAY'S PROMISE

The LORD directs our steps, so why try to understand everything along the way? —PROVERBS 20:24

TODAY'S THOUGHT

Life is less confusing when you realize that God is in control, not to manipulate you or to order you around but to assure you that this world is not random and chaotic. If it were, life would be meaningless. But since God *is* in control, you can live a life of purpose that will make a difference for all eternity. How wonderful to know that even when life seems meaningless, God has the answers.

TODAY'S PLAN

Where are you most confused? How can knowing God is in control help?

ADVICE

TODAY'S PROMISE

Get all the advice and instruction you can, so you will be wise the rest of your life. —PROVERBS 19:20

TODAY'S THOUGHT

One aspect of wisdom is recognizing your own inadequacies. Foolishness is thinking you have none. Good friends can bring perspective, new information, and experience to whatever challenges and problems you face. No one is wise enough to anticipate all the possibilities of a situation or to grasp all the issues related to a problem. The right counsel brings you wisdom that you can apply for a lifetime.

TODAY'S PLAN

Who can be a good advisor to you?

GOALS

TODAY'S PROMISE

*I cry out to God Most High, to God who will
fulfill his purpose for me.* —PSALM 57:2

TODAY'S THOUGHT

Purpose in life comes from knowing God and
doing his will. The ultimate goal in life is not to
achieve the goals you want, but to do what God
has planned for you to do. God created you for
a purpose and promises to fulfill his intentions
in your life when you truly want him to.

TODAY'S PLAN

*What are some goals you can set to help you find your God-given
purpose and fulfill it?*

IMAGINATION

TODAY'S PROMISE

The LORD will comfort Israel again and have
pity. . . . Her desert will blossom like Eden, her
barren wilderness like the garden of the LORD.
Joy and gladness will be found there. Songs of
thanksgiving will fill the air. —ISAIAH 51:3

TODAY'S THOUGHT

Faith grows when you recall God's great acts
in the Bible and across the ages and trust that
he will continue to perform great acts for
his people today and in the future. Use your
imagination to let God's promised hope of new
and eternal life come alive in your mind. God
promises that when he transforms this old earth
into a new one, the curse of sin will be gone.
Imagine a life without the curse, and have
faith that it will happen.

TODAY'S PLAN

Imagine a world free from the curse of sin. What do you
see yourself doing there?

PANIC

TODAY'S PROMISE

When the earth quakes and its people live in turmoil, I am the one who keeps its foundations firm.

—Psalm 75:3

God is our refuge and strength, always ready to help in times of trouble. So we will not fear when earthquakes come and the mountains crumble into the sea.

—Psalm 46:1-2

TODAY'S THOUGHT

Panic is physically and emotionally paralyzing when worry and fear meet an instant crisis. You may have had no time to prepare for it and are too frozen with fear to deal with it. If you haven't prepared for it, you won't be able to deal well with it when it hits. The closer you are to God, the more you can tap into his strength and peace when panic strikes. Then you will have a clear head and be able to act with purpose.

TODAY'S PLAN

How do you deal with panic?

SALVATION

TODAY'S PROMISE

Because of Christ and our faith in him, we can now come boldly and confidently into God's presence.

—EPHESIANS 3:12

TODAY'S THOUGHT

If you have a free pass to an event, you would not hesitate to enter. You are given the privilege of admission based on the generosity of the giver. Your faith in Jesus Christ is God's free pass into his presence. When you put your trust in Jesus Christ, you can enter God's presence with confidence.

TODAY'S PLAN

Have you accepted God's free pass to live forever in heaven with him?

COMMITMENT

TODAY'S PROMISE

[Jesus said,] "I am the vine; you are the branches. Those who remain in me, and I in them, will produce much fruit. For apart from me you can do nothing. . . . You didn't choose me. I chose you. I appointed you to go and produce lasting fruit, so that the Father will give you whatever you ask for, using my name."
—JOHN 15:5, 16

TODAY'S THOUGHT

God promises that commitment to him makes you productive in service. You can be assured of this because God chose you and appointed you to serve him and work for him in a unique way. When you're committed to him, your work will be most productive in what really matters. Be committed to him so that you can accomplish the many things he created you to do.

TODAY'S PLAN

Where can greater commitment make you more productive for God?

MERCY

TODAY'S PROMISE

You, O LORD, are a God of compassion and mercy, slow to get angry and filled with unfailing love and faithfulness. —PSALM 86:15

TODAY'S THOUGHT

Mercy is one of the best feelings in the world. The world can be a bad enough place sometimes, but without mercy it would be unbearable. God not only gives you mercy every time you sin, but he also forgives you and shows you fresh mercy every day, 365 days a year. Receive his mercy with a grateful heart and commit yourself to extending more mercy to others.

TODAY'S PLAN

Who might need to receive mercy today instead of judgment?

COURAGE

TODAY'S PROMISE

What shall we say about such wonderful things as these? If God is for us, who can ever be against us? Since he did not spare even his own Son but gave him up for us all, won't he also give us everything else?

—ROMANS 8:31-32

TODAY'S THOUGHT

Since God gave up his own Son to give you eternal life and freedom from sin, won't he also give you the strength and resources you need to face your fears and troubles? God wants to see his children overcome. With almighty God on your side, you can have the courage to face anything or anyone.

TODAY'S PLAN

Where could you use more courage? Does it help to picture God right by your side, wanting what is best for you?

HOSPITALITY

TODAY'S PROMISE

*"When you put on a luncheon or a banquet," [Jesus]
said, "don't invite your friends, brothers, relatives,
and rich neighbors. For they will invite you back,
and that will be your only reward. Instead, invite
the poor, the crippled, the lame, and the blind.
Then at the resurrection of the righteous, God
will reward you for inviting those who could not
repay you."* —LUKE 14:12-14

TODAY'S THOUGHT

Although some are certainly gifted with hospitality, you are called to practice hospitality as best
you can, for it is a basic act of kindness to others, and it encourages and comforts them.

Hospitality is also an expression of gratitude
to God for what he has done for you. God
blesses you when your hospitality focuses on
encouraging and caring for others and on
presenting him to those around you.

TODAY'S PLAN

In what ways are you practicing hospitality?

BLESSINGS

TODAY'S PROMISE

All praise to God, the Father of our Lord Jesus Christ, who has blessed us with every spiritual blessing in the heavenly realms because we are united with Christ. —EPHESIANS 1:3

TODAY'S THOUGHT

If you want God's blessings just so you can live an easier, more comfortable life, then you don't understand the nature of God's blessings. When you live to please God, you understand that all you are and all you have is a gift from him, to be used by him to bless others. Then, as your desire to serve God grows, you will find yourself in the middle of a rushing stream of God's blessings, to be used to refresh others.

TODAY'S PLAN

What can you do to receive more of the blessing of God?

TIME

TODAY'S PROMISE

Teach us to realize the brevity of life, so that we may grow in wisdom.

—PSALM 90:12

TODAY'S THOUGHT

Believe it or not, the best way to have the time you need is to devote time to God for worship and to yourself for rest. Devoting time to God gives you spiritual refreshment and the opportunity to hear his priorities for you. Devoting time to rest gives you physical refreshment and the energy to do what you are called to do. When you make these two times a priority, you will have the time to do everything you really need to do.

TODAY'S PLAN

Are you spending enough time with God to discover how he wants you to use it?

ASHAMED

TODAY'S PROMISE

The LORD is my light and my salvation—so why should I be afraid? The LORD is my fortress, protecting me from danger, so why should I tremble?

—PSALM 27:1

TODAY'S THOUGHT

Do you sometimes feel ashamed of your faith when others disapprove? Since your value is determined by God's approval, not by the approval or disapproval of others, your purpose is to please God, who made you and redeemed you, no matter what others may think of you. When you focus on pleasing God, you won't feel ashamed when others disapprove of your faith.

TODAY'S PLAN

How do you respond when others disapprove of your faith?

JOY

TODAY'S PROMISE

Praise the LORD! How joyful are those who fear the LORD and delight in obeying his commands.

—PSALM 112:1

TODAY'S THOUGHT

It seems ironic that the more you fear the Lord, the more joyful you will be. But the Bible says that to fear the Lord (to respect him so much you want to obey him) is the way to wisdom. Wisdom helps you make good choices that bring joy and happiness, and helps you avoid harmful choices that bring misery.

TODAY'S PLAN

Are you making the kind of life choices that bring real joy?

FEELINGS

TODAY'S PROMISE

Pour out your heart to him, for God is our refuge.

—PSALM 62:8

TODAY'S THOUGHT

God is your safe place, your hiding place, where you can honestly and safely pour out your heart and be assured that God not only hears your prayers but also understands your feelings.

TODAY'S PLAN

How safe do you feel pouring out your heart to God? How might you feel even more safe doing so?

BURDENS

TODAY'S PROMISE

The LORD helps the fallen and lifts those bent beneath their loads. —PSALM 145:14

TODAY'S THOUGHT

God's hot line is always open. There is never a busy signal, and he is never too pre-occupied with anything—even managing the world—to listen to your every need. God has both a listening ear and a caring heart.

TODAY'S PLAN

How can you find comfort when you're weighed down by burdens?

CONFESSION

TODAY'S PROMISE

Confess your sins to each other and pray for each other so that you may be healed. —JAMES 5:16

TODAY'S THOUGHT

It can be healing to confess sin to one another, especially if others are committed to praying for you, encouraging you, and supporting you as you seek restoration. It is also important to confess sin to those whom you have wronged. To have this kind of loving support system around you keeps you spiritually healthy and strong against temptation.

TODAY'S PLAN

Where are you getting help with your need to confess?

STEWARDSHIP

TODAY'S PROMISE

The earth is the LORD's, and everything in it. The world and all its people belong to him. —PSALM 24:1

Each of us will give a personal account to God.
—ROMANS 14:12

TODAY'S THOUGHT

If a friend loaned you her new car, you'd make every effort to care for it and use it well. Everything you have is on loan to you from God; he owns it all and he is letting you use it. Make sure you are a good steward of all he has entrusted in your care because someday you will have to give it back to him and account for what you did with what he gave you.

TODAY'S PLAN

What is your attitude toward the things God has trusted you to care for? How can you be a better steward of earth's resources? Of your relationships? Of your possessions?

JULY

PROMISES

TODAY'S PROMISE

God is not a man, so he does not lie. He is not human, so he does not change his mind. Has he ever spoken and failed to act? Has he ever promised and not carried it through? —NUMBERS 23:19

TODAY'S THOUGHT

Marriage vows are breathtaking in beauty and boldness and are intended to be binding "as long as we both shall live." Yet divorce statistics prove that even these promises are not taken very seriously. But God's promises are anchored in his unchanging character and steadfast love. In fact, God has never broken a promise. Where even our most heartfelt promises sometimes falter, God's word is his promise and never fails.

TODAY'S PLAN

If you knew people who followed through on 100 percent of what they promised, how would that affect your level of trust in them? How much do you trust God?

KEEP GOING

TODAY'S PROMISE

Though I fall, I will rise again. Though I sit in darkness, the LORD will be my light. —MICAH 7:8

We are hunted down, but never abandoned by God. We get knocked down, but we are not destroyed.

—2 CORINTHIANS 4:9

TODAY'S THOUGHT

When you've been knocked down, you can get up again because God promises to help you rise up if you let him. Many of life's inspiring success stories come from people who failed many times, but never gave up. Most important, never give up on your relationship with God, who promises you ultimate victory through eternal life.

TODAY'S PLAN

Have you been having trouble getting up again after a recent failure?

COMMUNICATION

Long ago God spoke many times and in many ways to our ancestors through the prophets. And now in these final days, he has spoken to us through his Son. —HEBREWS 1:1-2

We like to keep in touch because it is vital to the quality and success of a relationship, whether marriage, friendship, family, or business. The same principal applies to your relationship with God. As you communicate with him and learn to listen as he communicates with you, you will experience real growth in your spiritual life.

When was the last time you felt in touch with God? How much time do you spend communicating with him?

FREEDOM

TODAY'S PROMISE

He gave his life to purchase freedom for everyone. This is the message God gave to the world at just the right time. —1 TIMOTHY 2:6

TODAY'S THOUGHT

Freedom is wonderful. It allows you to make your own choices, but it should motivate you to choose to live in such in a way that you won't lose your freedom. God offers freedom to all people—freedom from eternal death and the rights and privileges of being his children forever. That is God's good news. God doesn't want you to feel guilty about being free; he wants you to enjoy your freedom and make the most of it.

TODAY'S PLAN

Does the freedom God gives you motivate you to serve him well?

IMPOSSIBLE

TODAY'S PROMISE

Jesus looked at them intently and said, "Humanly speaking, it is impossible. But with God everything is possible."
—MATTHEW 19:26

TODAY'S THOUGHT

There should be no doubt that God specializes in doing the impossible. The end of your abilities is the beginning of his. The God who spoke all creation into being can do miracles for you. But you must believe he can and that he wants to. Your impossibilities are God's opportunities.

TODAY'S PLAN

If you gave your biggest problems to God, how might he make them opportunities to do something big through you?

AFFECTION

TODAY'S PROMISE

Long ago the LORD said to Israel: "I have loved you, my people, with an everlasting love. With unfailing love I have drawn you to myself."

—JEREMIAH 31:3

TODAY'S THOUGHT

God desires a daily and eternal relationship with you, and continually pursues you with his love. His primary desire is to draw you to himself in a relationship that will last forever in love and security.

TODAY'S PLAN

Are you allowing yourself to be drawn toward God, or are you running from him?

GOSSIP

TODAY'S PROMISE

A gossip goes around telling secrets, but those who are trustworthy can keep a confidence. —PROVERBS 11:13

TODAY'S THOUGHT

What comes out of your mouth shows what is in your heart. Your words show what kind of person you really are. Gossip, criticism, flattery, lying, and profanity are not only "word" problems but also "heart problems." Being more careful about the words you choose to use isn't enough. First, you need a change of heart—and then good, kind, and healing words will follow, and you will be trusted by others.

TODAY'S PLAN

Are you having "word" problems?

POWER OF GOD

TODAY'S PROMISE

Instead, give yourselves completely to God, for you were dead, but now you have new life. So use your whole body as an instrument to do what is right for the glory of God. Sin is no longer your master, for you no longer live under the requirements of the law. Instead, you live under the freedom of God's grace. —ROMANS 6:13-14

TODAY'S THOUGHT

One of Satan's great lies is that heredity, environment, and circumstances excuse you from responsibility for sin. But God is more powerful than anything that seeks to control you. When you call on his power, God breaks the chains that hold you and sets you free.

TODAY'S PLAN

Are you tapping into enough of God's power to free you from slavery to sin?

BOREDOM

TODAY'S PROMISE

Our great desire is that you will keep on loving others as long as life lasts, in order to make certain that what you hope for will come true. Then you will not become spiritually dull and indifferent.

—HEBREWS 6:11-12

TODAY'S THOUGHT

Being a Christian can seem boring—too much "do this, and don't do that." But those who grasp what the Christian life is all about find it full and exciting. If you become bored in your Christian life, it may be because you are not making yourself available to God and asking him to pour his blessings through you to others.

TODAY'S PLAN

How might God want to work through you to accomplish something special? Act on that, and you will not be bored.

MEDITATION

You will keep in perfect peace all who trust in you, all whose thoughts are fixed on you! —ISAIAH 26:3

Meditation goes beyond the study of God to true communion with him. Remember God first thing in the morning, and fall asleep with him on your mind. Meditate on God as the source of the hope you think you've lost. Think about him with a thankful heart when you have plenty, for you will need to rely on him when you have little. Weave him into the fabric of your life so that you, your children, and your grandchildren will be trained to love God.

What are some ways that you can remind yourself to think about God during the day?

COMPASSION

TODAY'S PROMISE

When the Lord saw her, his heart overflowed with compassion. "Don't cry!" he said. —LUKE 7:13

The LORD is good to everyone. He showers compassion on all his creation. —PSALM 145:9

TODAY'S THOUGHT

A lack of compassion hurts those whom God has placed in your life. It also causes your heart to grow cold. A cold heart is a dead heart. If you find yourself thinking mostly about your own needs and desires, your heart is losing the compassion that makes you effective for God and spiritually and emotionally healthy.

TODAY'S PLAN

What can you do to determine if you are becoming more or less compassionate?

SORROW

TODAY'S PROMISE

Weeping may last through the night, but joy comes with the morning.
—PSALM 30:5

TODAY'S THOUGHT

One of the most common denominators of human experience is sorrow. Whether predictable and necessary or seemingly random and tragic, the losses of life affect us profoundly. The Bible acknowledges that sorrow and grief are part of life. But Scripture does not give sorrow the last word. God redeems our losses with his promises of comfort and hope in a future where sorrow will be no more.

TODAY'S PLAN

What have been some of the greatest losses in your life? How might God's promise of hope help sustain you until he redeems those tragedies?

GOODNESS

TODAY'S PROMISE

A good person produces good things from the treasury of a good heart, and an evil person produces evil things from the treasury of an evil heart.

—MATTHEW 12:35

TODAY'S THOUGHT

What you say and do opens the window to your soul and shows the world around you what is inside. If you have practiced goodness from God, the world will see treasures within. If you haven't, the window of your speech and actions will reveal the impoverishment of your soul.

TODAY'S PLAN

Are others seeing a treasury of good coming from inside of you?

PEACE

TODAY'S PROMISE

There will be glory and honor and peace from God for all who do good. —ROMANS 2:10

TODAY'S THOUGHT

Peace with God comes from living the way you were created to live. That happens when you develop a relationship with your Creator and live by the standards he has written in his Word, the Bible. When you set aside a lifestyle of ignoring and neglecting him, and work toward a lifestyle that honors and obeys him, you will experience God's peace as your mind, heart, and actions get into sync with his.

TODAY'S PLAN

Are you at peace with God?

DECISIONS

TODAY'S PROMISE

Who are those who fear the LORD? He will show them the path they should choose. —PSALM 25:12

TODAY'S THOUGHT

Pray for God to give you the desire to want his guidance, and then to follow it when he makes it clear. Then you will be able to make decisions that please him. God doesn't want to hide his will from you—he's not playing games with you. He wants to give you guidance; you just need to ask and then listen and respond when he speaks.

TODAY'S PLAN

How often do you take the time to really listen when you ask for guidance? In what ways can you make yourself more aware of God's guidance?

RECONCILIATION

TODAY'S PROMISE

God was in Christ, reconciling the world to himself, no longer counting people's sins against them. . . . We speak for Christ when we plead, "Come back to God!" For God made Christ, who never sinned, to be the offering for our sin, so that we could be made right with God through Christ.

—2 CORINTHIANS 5:19-21

TODAY'S THOUGHT

Reconciliation is possible only when one party makes the first move: a hand extended, a phone call, a word of forgiveness. In the same way, sin causes an uncrossable chasm between us and God. Although it is we who need to be reconciled, God made the first move. He extended not just his hand, not just words, but his Son to bridge the chasm between himself and us.

TODAY'S PLAN

God has made the first move to reconcile you to him. Have you responded?

FRUITFULNESS

TODAY'S PROMISE

[Jesus said,] "[My Father] prunes the branches that do bear fruit so they will produce even more. You have already been pruned and purified by the message I have given you. Remain in me, and I will remain in you. For a branch cannot produce fruit if it is severed from the vine, and you cannot be fruitful unless you remain in me." —JOHN 15:2-4

TODAY'S THOUGHT

Sometimes it may feel as though God is taking things away from you, but what he is really doing is cutting away things that keep you from producing fruit. God prunes you to make you a person whose life is bountiful with good fruit.

TODAY'S PLAN

Do you feel as though God is cutting away parts of your life? How can you submit yourself to his care and look for ways to produce fruit?

INSIGNIFICANCE

TODAY'S PROMISE

What is the price of two sparrows—one copper coin? But not a single sparrow can fall to the ground without your Father knowing it. And the very hairs on your head are all numbered. So don't be afraid; you are more valuable to God than a whole flock of sparrows.

—MATTHEW 10:29-31

TODAY'S THOUGHT

Within every human heart lies a hunger for significance. We want our lives to count, to make a difference, to be worth something. Yet many of us carry deep feelings of insignificance. Our lives and aspirations are dominated not by our abilities but by our inabilities. Everywhere we look we see others who are more successful, more gifted, more this, more that. The Bible, however, points out that every person holds great value. You *are* significant, not for what you can accomplish on your own but because God loves you and promises to accomplish much through you.

TODAY'S PLAN

How can your day change knowing that God sees great value and unlimited potential in you?

CHANGE

TODAY'S PROMISE

We know that God causes everything to work together for the good of those who love God and are called according to his purpose for them. —ROMANS 8:28

TODAY'S THOUGHT

Sometimes change seems to be for the worse. At those times, you may feel as if you're going to fall apart. When such change occurs, remember that traumatic, unpredictable, and unfair change never trumps God's will. Nothing takes him by surprise. No change occurs that he does not allow and that he cannot redeem.

TODAY'S PLAN

When you are surprised by change, how can you remember that God is not?

OPPORTUNITIES

TODAY'S PROMISE

We ask God to give you complete knowledge of his will and to give you spiritual wisdom and understanding. —COLOSSIANS 1:9

The earnest prayer of a righteous person has great power and produces wonderful results. —JAMES 5:16

TODAY'S THOUGHT

Do you notice and respond to opportunities as they become available? Prayer is a way to stay alert and on the watch for how God will move in your life. Prayer keeps you connected to him and spiritually sensitive so that you can recognize his voice and actions and discern whether or not an opportunity is from him. Left to yourself, you may miss much, but when God's Spirit connects with your spirit you will hear and see much more.

TODAY'S PLAN

Are you staying well-connected to God so you can hear his voice when he calls?

FORGIVENESS

TODAY'S PROMISE

Oh, what joy for those whose disobedience is forgiven, whose sins are put out of sight. —ROMANS 4:7

TODAY'S THOUGHT

God's love is his motivation for his forgiveness. He wants a relationship with you more than anything, and he is happy to forgive you for any sin, no matter how terrible, if you simply long for a relationship with him and seek his forgiveness. The best part of receiving God's forgiveness is experiencing the joy of your restored relationship with him.

TODAY'S PLAN

Have you asked for God's forgiveness and restored your relationship with him?

SACRIFICE

TODAY'S PROMISE

[Jesus] said to the crowd, "If any of you wants to be my follower, you must turn from your selfish ways, take up your cross daily, and follow me. If you try to hang on to your life, you will lose it. But if you give up your life for my sake, you will save it." —LUKE 9:23-24

TODAY'S THOUGHT

A short-term sacrifice is often necessary to produce a long-term gain. We refrain from buying the latest gadget in order to save our money for something more important. A parent sacrifices time and energy so that a child can experience success later in life. An athlete endures much pain in order to win an Olympic medal later. So it is with our faith. Following Christ often calls for sacrifice in the short run—but that sacrifice produces blessings that will last for eternity.

TODAY'S PLAN

What will your salvation cost you? Are you willing to sacrifice now in order to gain an eternal reward?

ENCOURAGEMENT

TODAY'S PROMISE

Humble yourselves before the Lord, and he will lift you up in honor.
—JAMES 4:10

TODAY'S THOUGHT

Humility is essential in receiving encouragement. When you're feeling discouraged, do you indulge in discontent or do you humbly put yourself at God's feet, admitting your need for his comfort? Are you willing to accept whatever comes from his hand? To be encouraged, you must want help, be willing to accept it, and humbly receive it with gratitude.

TODAY'S PLAN

Do you make it difficult for others to give you encouragement? How can you open yourself up to truly being encouraged today?

PATIENCE

TODAY'S PROMISE

This vision is for a future time. . . . If it seems slow in coming, wait patiently, for it will surely take place. It will not be delayed. —HABAKKUK 2:3

TODAY'S THOUGHT

Restlessness is the result of losing patience with God while waiting for his plans to be fulfilled. Patiently waiting for God can actually give you an attitude of anticipation for each new day. If God is going to do what is best for you, then his plan for you will be accomplished on his schedule, not yours. If you keep that in mind, you can wake up each day anticipating what good thing he has in store for you at just the right time.

TODAY'S PLAN

How can you change your attitude so that needing to wait patiently is something you can look forward to?

CONFLICT

TODAY'S PROMISE

Blessed are those who fear to do wrong, but the stubborn are headed for serious trouble. —PROVERBS 28:14

TODAY'S THOUGHT

Most of us experience inner conflict. We may have given our lives to follow Christ, but our old nature still exists. We don't want to do wrong, yet we often do. We know the attitudes and behavior that Christ desires, but we also know how hard it is to live that way. Ironically, this kind of tension shows that your conscience is still sensitive to sin and that you truly desire to do what is right. It is that attitude that causes God to call you blessed.

TODAY'S PLAN

Are you truly concerned with doing what is right and good in God's eyes? Then you can have peace that you are blessed by God.

PRAYER

TODAY'S PROMISE

The eyes of the Lord watch over those who do right, and his ears are open to their prayers. —1 PETER 3:12

TODAY'S THOUGHT

Sometimes it may feel as if your prayers are bouncing off the ceiling. Is God paying attention? Perhaps the more important question is, Are *you* paying attention to God's response? God responds to you because he is loving and good. And it's his nature to give good things to his people. Just remember that he knows what is good for you. When you pray, be alert and watch for God's response, even if it isn't what you expected. Be content when his answer is "no" or "wait awhile." In fact, be at peace because you know he has better things in store for you.

TODAY'S PLAN

If God says no, are you interpreting that as silence or as a loving answer to move you in a better direction?

FAVOR WITH GOD

TODAY'S PROMISE

Never let loyalty and kindness leave you! Tie them around your neck as a reminder. Write them deep within your heart. Then you will find favor with both God and people, and you will earn a good reputation.
—PROVERBS 3:3-4

TODAY'S THOUGHT

The human heart longs for loyalty and kindness. To be noticed and treated as special causes you to behave in a different way. Treat others with loyalty and kindness, and the Bible promises that you will win not only the favor of God but the favor of others as well.

TODAY'S PLAN

To whom can you show loyalty and kindness today, even though they don't deserve it? Try it and experience a breakthrough in your relationships.

PROTECTION

TODAY'S PROMISE

He has not ignored or belittled the suffering of the needy. He has not turned his back on them, but has listened to their cries for help. —PSALM 22:24

TODAY'S THOUGHT

Suffering is not a sign that God doesn't care; it is simply a fact of life in this fallen world. If God took away everyone's suffering, we would not need him or desire heaven. More significantly, we would probably follow God for a magic cure rather than because of our need for salvation. God uses suffering to get people's attention and draw them to him. Although the Bible never promises a life free from pain, it does promise that God is with you and listens to your cries for help.

TODAY'S PLAN

Can you look beyond today's pain and rejoice that God will protect you from pain and evil for eternity?

CONFIDENCE

Oh, the joys of those who trust the LORD, who have no confidence in the proud or in those who worship idols.

—PSALM 40:4

TODAY'S THOUGHT

Confidence in God is often misguided. You may think that your faith would be stronger if he gave you things that made your life easier and more comfortable, but you're not setting your sights high enough. The things you want often distract you from the God you need and long for. Your confidence comes not by getting what you want but by relying on God to give you what you really need.

TODAY'S PLAN

Catalog the things you ask God for. What are they? What could you ask God to reveal about himself to you today?

PAST

TODAY'S PROMISE

He was pierced for our rebellion, crushed for our sins. He was beaten so we could be whole. He was whipped so we could be healed. All of us, like sheep, have strayed away. We have left God's paths to follow our own. Yet the LORD laid on him the sins of us all.
—ISAIAH 53:5-6

TODAY'S THOUGHT

It is impossible to follow God and still hold on to old habits of sin. Think of trying to walk in two directions at once! If you are hanging on to sinful attitudes or habits from your past, you are not just standing still; you are deliberately walking away from God. He invites you to turn around and walk toward him so you can experience the life he wants to give you; the life Christ died to give you.

TODAY'S PLAN

How might your past be pulling you away from God? How can you turn around and walk toward him?

ATTITUDE

TODAY'S PROMISE

"Why are you so angry?" the LORD asked Cain. "Why do you look so dejected? You will be accepted if you do what is right. But if you refuse to do what is right, then watch out! Sin is crouching at the door, eager to control you." —GENESIS 4:6-7

TODAY'S THOUGHT

When your actions focus on serving God, you will begin to develop an eternal perspective about life that changes the way you look at the world. The bottom line is this: life is more about how you react to your circumstances than what actually happens to you. Your attitude makes the difference between being content and happy or discontent and miserable.

TODAY'S PLAN

How do you react to negative circumstances?

AUGUST

RESISTING TEMPTATION

TODAY'S PROMISE

Do not let sin control the way you live; do not give in to sinful desires.　　　　　　　　　　—ROMANS 6:12

Humble yourselves before God. Resist the devil, and he will flee from you.　　　　　　　　　　—JAMES 4:7

TODAY'S THOUGHT

Weak spots are joints in your spiritual armor at which the enemy takes aim, the areas in which you compromise your convictions, even for a few moments. It is those areas of weakness where you must ask God to cover your vulnerable spots with his strength. It is a disaster to discover your weak spots in the heat of the battle; you must discover them before the fighting begins. With a strategy to protect your points of vulnerability, you will be prepared when the enemy attacks.

TODAY'S PLAN

Are you aware of your weak spots, where Satan will attack and tempt you?

CHURCH

TODAY'S PROMISE

[Jesus said,] "Where two or three gather together as my followers, I am there among them." —MATTHEW 18:20

TODAY'S THOUGHT

Even though God lives in the heart of every believer, he also lives in the community of the church. When the church is gathered together, it meets God in a special way. Just like actually being at a concert or sports event is so much more exciting, participating with other believers in worshiping God is so much more meaningful because you experience the presence and power of God in ways you never could on your own.

TODAY'S PLAN

Is your church community helping you experience God in a transforming way?

REPENTANCE

TODAY'S PROMISE

*Repent of your sins and turn to God, for the
Kingdom of Heaven is near.* —MATTHEW 3:2

TODAY'S THOUGHT

Have you ever been driving and suddenly real-
ized you were going the wrong way on a one-way
street? What do you do? You make a U-turn and
change direction as soon as you can. The Bible
calls the wrong way "sin." Repentance is making a commitment, with God's help, to change
your life's direction. Although not a popu-
lar concept these days, repentance is essential,
because it is the only way to arrive at your desired
destination—right standing with God now and
eternity in heaven.

TODAY'S PLAN

*Have you recognized that repentance requires that you
make a change in the direction of your life?*

HONESTY

TODAY'S PROMISE

Don't lie to each other, for you have stripped off your old sinful nature and all its wicked deeds. Put on your new nature, and be renewed as you learn to know your Creator and become like him.

—COLOSSIANS 3:9–10

TODAY'S THOUGHT

There are times when people need to hear the straight truth rather than a pep talk. Often people seek advice from those who will confirm their own sinful desires and make excuses for their destructive or unhealthy behaviors. But your words of truth might be just what someone needs to hear in order to turn from sin. So don't be afraid to speak the truth. If your words are spoken with Christlike love, the Spirit can use them to touch the other person's heart.

TODAY'S PLAN

Who do you know who needs to be confronted—gently but firmly—with God's truth?

FOCUSED

TODAY'S PROMISE

We can rejoice, too, when we run into problems and trials, for we know that they help us develop endurance. And endurance develops strength of character, and character strengthens our confident hope of salvation.

—ROMANS 5:3-4

TODAY'S THOUGHT

Just as focusing on a fixed point in the distance helps you travel in a straighter line, focusing on the eternal horizon—your ultimate destination of heaven—will lead you straight to your goal of living with Jesus forever where there is no pain or sorrow or suffering. As you stay focused on your eternal goal, you will be able to put life's disappointments in perspective.

TODAY'S PLAN

What are some practical ways that you can turn your focus beyond your current disappointment to your eternal hope?

LETTING GO

Refusing to accept God's way, they cling to their own way of getting right with God by trying to keep the law. For Christ has already accomplished the purpose for which the law was given. As a result, all who believe in him are made right with God.

—ROMANS 10:3-4

Out of a natural desire to control your own life comes the idea that you can earn your way to heaven. But salvation and eternal life are gifts from God—you can do nothing to earn them. When you stop trying to control your destiny, you will gain a sense of freedom because you will have assurance that God has already promised you a perfect future. Letting go doesn't mean you don't do your best; it means that after you have done your best, you step back and trust God to complete the work he started.

Are you still trying to control your future?

JEALOUSY

TODAY'S PROMISE

Don't envy sinners, but always continue to fear the LORD. You will be rewarded for this; your hope will not be disappointed. —PROVERBS 23:17-18

TODAY'S THOUGHT

Jealousy reveals selfishness: You want what someone else has and resent the blessings and joy of others, especially those who you may feel don't deserve it. The inability to rejoice in another's success or blessings limits your own capacity for joy. The cure for jealousy is gratitude and satisfaction in doing what pleases God. God promises to satisfy the hopes of those who find their contentment from loving and serving him.

TODAY'S PLAN

What makes you really content? Was God part of your answer?

AFFIRMATION

TODAY'S PROMISE

You bless the godly, O L{\scriptsize ORD}; you surround them with your shield of love. —PSALM 5:12

TODAY'S THOUGHT

In ancient times, shields were the strongest kind of protection, designed to keep an arrow from piercing one's body and causing deadly injury. God says his love is like a shield that surrounds you and stops arrows of doubt, temptation, and confusion that Satan shoots at you. What an affirmation! God loves you so much that he promises to shield you from the enemy's strongest attacks. God's love does not always provide physical protection, but God is always protecting your soul, which is so precious to him.

TODAY'S PLAN

As you go about your day, can you picture God's love as a shield around you?

RELEASE

TODAY'S PROMISE

The word of God is alive and powerful. It is sharper than the sharpest two-edged sword, cutting between soul and spirit, between joint and marrow. It exposes our innermost thoughts and desires. —HEBREWS 4:12

TODAY'S THOUGHT

God's Word is the light that reveals the sin in you that needs to be exposed. Just as light extinguishes darkness, God's Word shines light into the dark corners of your life, revealing sin so that you can extinguish it. Only when you stop hiding your sins where others can't see them can you be released from their power to control you.

TODAY'S PLAN

What sins have you been hiding? Are you prepared to let God's Word reveal them?

PERFECTION

TODAY'S PROMISE

I don't mean to say that I have already achieved these things or that I have already reached perfection. But I press on to possess that perfection for which Christ Jesus first possessed me. —PHILIPPIANS 3:12

TODAY'S THOUGHT

Most of us wish we could be perfect in some way. We want to be the perfect spouse or parent, perform flawlessly, or be supremely skilled or accurate. Life on earth will always be a struggle between our longing to be perfect and the reality of our sinful humanness. What we really long for is heaven, where perfection is natural. God understands our longing for perfection and sent his Son, Jesus, to accomplish what we could not. Jesus exchanged the burdens of our humanness for his perfect holiness so that we can be blameless before God and one day be perfect in heaven.

TODAY'S PLAN

Are you longing for heaven?

CARE/CARING

TODAY'S PROMISE

If God cares so wonderfully for wildflowers that are here today and thrown into the fire tomorrow, he will certainly care for you. —MATTHEW 6:30

TODAY'S THOUGHT

God's love for you began before you were born, continues throughout your life, and extends through eternity. Since he created you to have a relationship with him, he cares about every detail of your life. He knows all your troubles and hurts and offers to take care of you during them. Will you let him?

TODAY'S PLAN

How much do you trust God to really care for you?

FULFILLMENT

TODAY'S PROMISE

The thief's purpose is to steal and kill and destroy. [Christ's] purpose is to give them a rich and satisfying life.

—JOHN 10:10

TODAY'S THOUGHT

Within all humans is the God-given desire for our lives to amount to something. This desire drives some to become famous, attain a prestigious position, or be recognized for some accomplishment. But these are no guarantee that a life really matters. Serving God is what gives significance to life because you are serving the One who created you for a purpose. Find out his purpose for you, and your life will be rich and satisfying. In the world's eyes, you may never be much of anything, but in God's eyes your life will be full and invaluable.

TODAY'S PLAN

How are you pursuing a rich and satisfying life?

MENTORING

TODAY'S PROMISE

You have heard me teach things that have been confirmed by many reliable witnesses. Now teach these truths to other trustworthy people who will be able to pass them on to others. . . . The Lord will help you understand all these things.

—2 TIMOTHY 2:2, 7

TODAY'S THOUGHT

A mentoring relationship has the specific purpose of teaching and learning. Good mentors commit to building a relationship with someone younger or with less life experience. Through this relationship, a mentor shares wisdom, life experience, and support in hopes of helping their mentee learn and grow. Similarly, Christ sent us the Holy Spirit as our spiritual mentor. The Holy Spirit helps us build a relationship with God and guides us into wisdom, maturity, and understanding.

TODAY'S PLAN

Are you mentoring someone and passing along the wisdom God gave you?

GOOD-BYES

TODAY'S PROMISE

If I ride the wings of the morning, if I dwell by the farthest oceans, even there your hand will guide me, and your strength will support me. —PSALM 139:9-10

TODAY'S THOUGHT

Whether we wave good-bye to our children each morning as they walk to school or shed tears of grief as we bury a parent, good-byes are hard. Farewells will always be part of this life. But God is the constant we can always count on. You will never have to say good-bye to him, and he will never leave you. No matter where you go, even across the farthest oceans, God is with you, guiding and comforting you. And when you arrive in heaven, all the farewells will be over, and there will be only sweet greetings.

TODAY'S PLAN

Have you thought about the joy of one day never having to say good-bye again?

AUGUST 15

CONSCIENCE

I always try to maintain a clear conscience before God and all people. —ACTS 24:16

My conscience is clear, but that doesn't prove I'm right. It is the LORD himself who will examine me and decide. —1 CORINTHIANS 4:4

TODAY'S THOUGHT

Your conscience is God's gift that helps you understand whether or not you are in line with God's will. But if you don't care for your conscience, it can malfunction. When your conscience is working faithfully, it will activate your heart and mind to know right from wrong. Are you having trouble deciding what is right? If so, it may be an indication that your conscience is not as sharp as it should be.

TODAY'S PLAN

Ask the Holy Spirit to teach you through God's holy Word and to sharpen and resensitize your conscience.

WEALTH

TODAY'S PROMISE

*Those who love money will never have enough.
How meaningless to think that wealth brings true
happiness!* —ECCLESIASTES 5:10

TODAY'S THOUGHT

The pursuit of wealth can easily deceive you into
thinking, *If only I had a little more, I would be content.*
The Bible says that nothing could be further
from the truth. Always wanting more reflects a
materialistic attitude that always leads to discontent. Contentment is the result not of material
wealth but of spiritual wealth. The old cliché
"You can't take it with you" is true. So focus on
making spiritual investments. Keep an eternal
perspective and realize that real wealth lies not
in earthly possessions but in your true treasure—your relationship with God.

TODAY'S PLAN

How content are you with what you have?

FORGETTING

TODAY'S PROMISE

The same happens to all who forget God. The hopes of the godless evaporate. Their confidence hangs by a thread. They are leaning on a spider's web.

—JOB 8:13-14

TODAY'S THOUGHT

When you forget God, you have nothing left but sin and self, and how will those benefit you for your eternal future? Forgetting God leaves you with the consequences of sin without the benefits of God's mercy.

TODAY'S PLAN

Are you in danger of forgetting about God?

GRIEF

TODAY'S PROMISE

All praise to God, the Father of our Lord Jesus Christ. God is our merciful Father and the source of all comfort.
—2 CORINTHIANS 1:3

TODAY'S THOUGHT

Jesus suffered as deeply as any human could; he was acquainted with the bitterest grief. Because he can relate to your pain, and because of his great love for you, God understands and cares when you are hurting. His heart breaks along with yours. He is with you in your pain, and he promises to bless you in the middle of it.

TODAY'S PLAN

In what ways can you look for an extra measure of comfort from Jesus today?

SIN

Though we are overwhelmed by our sins, you forgive them all.
—PSALM 65:3

When a doctor correctly diagnoses a disease in your body, you don't accuse him of impinging on your freedom; rather, you are grateful because he will know how to treat the disease before it destroys your life. The Bible teaches that the disease of sin will destroy your life and lead to spiritual death if you don't treat it. Confessing your sins to God and turning away from them is the only way to be free from sin's power and your guilt.

Have you been freed from sin's power?

BLESSINGS

TODAY'S PROMISE

God blesses those who patiently endure testing and temptation. Afterward they will receive the crown of life that God has promised to those who love him.

—JAMES 1:12

TODAY'S THOUGHT

Blessings can come in strange ways. Sometimes great blessings come out of great trouble because these trials help you become spiritually mature, strengthen your faith, and most importantly deepen your relationship with the Lord, the greatest blessing of all. The testing itself is not a blessing, but God miraculously brings blessings even from hard times.

TODAY'S PLAN

What testing are you going through? What blessings can come from your hard times?

SENSITIVITY

TODAY'S PROMISE

Don't forget to do good and to share with those in need. These are the sacrifices that please God.

—HEBREWS 13:16

TODAY'S THOUGHT

God has equipped you in special ways to meet the needs of others around you. When you put aside your own agenda, listen carefully, and act thoughtfully, you are developing the kind of sensitive heart that is so attractive to God and that truly touches others right where they need it most.

TODAY'S PLAN

Who in your life needs a little more of your time and care?

CONVICTIONS

TODAY'S PROMISE

Let the Holy Spirit guide your lives. Then you won't be doing what your sinful nature craves. The sinful nature wants to do evil, which is just the opposite of what the Spirit wants. And the Spirit gives us desires that are the opposite of what the sinful nature desires. These two forces are constantly fighting each other, so you are not free to carry out your good intentions. —GALATIANS 5:16-17

TODAY'S THOUGHT

Every day you face choices between right and wrong, God's way or the way of the world. It takes practice to choose God's way, and it takes conviction to keep practicing. Be tenacious about not letting Satan gain any territory in your heart. Commit yourself to winning even the "little" battles. With the help of God's Holy Spirit, your life will be a great story of faith in God.

TODAY'S PLAN

What are you doing to develop stronger convictions?

WORTH

TODAY'S PROMISE

You made [people] only a little lower than God and crowned them with glory and honor. —PSALM 8:5

TODAY'S THOUGHT

What is the difference between paper plates and fine china? Paper plates are used once and thrown into the trash. But fine china is kept for generations and treated with the utmost care. We see fine china as more valuable than paper goods. When we use other people, we make them feel like paper plates—used and tossed away like trash. But the Bible tells us that all people have value. They are like fine china—a special creation with a special purpose—and they deserve to be treated with the utmost respect and care!

TODAY'S PLAN

How can you see everyone you meet as having equal worth in God's eyes?

AGING

TODAY'S PROMISE

Even in old age they will still produce fruit; they will remain vital and green. They will declare, "The LORD is just! He is my rock! There is no evil in him!" —PSALM 92:14-15

TODAY'S THOUGHT

God uses people of all ages to do his work. No one is too old or too young to have an impact for God. People look at outward appearance and age, but God looks at the heart. Godly hearts come to people of all ages, from little children to those in their golden years. Regardless of your age, use your life to affirm God's grace and goodness. Keep it vital and committed to serving him.

TODAY'S PLAN

In what areas would God consider your age an irrelevant issue?

WEAKNESSES

TODAY'S PROMISE

[Jesus said,] "Keep watch and pray, so that you will not give in to temptation. For the spirit is willing, but the body is weak." —MARK 14:38

TODAY'S THOUGHT

Often it is the moments when you think you're the strongest that you are most vulnerable. Faith in your own strength becomes a great weakness because you detach yourself from the greatest source of strength—God. The key is not external appearances but internal spiritual character. As you grow in spiritual maturity, you learn to recognize the weaknesses of your strengths and how to resist even the most powerful temptation.

TODAY'S PLAN

How can you become more aware of your strengths and weaknesses? How can you focus on your inward spiritual strength?

MIRACLES

TODAY'S PROMISE

*He rescues and saves his people; he performs
miraculous signs and wonders in the heavens
and on earth.* —DANIEL 6:27

TODAY'S THOUGHT

When you look for God, he shows himself in
miraculous ways: an awesome sunset, the restoration of a hopeless relationship, the birth
of a baby, the transforming work of love and
forgiveness, the specific call of God in your
life. God does the impossible to draw people to
him. He is able—and willing—to do the impossible in order to help you do his work. That means
no situation is hopeless. If you think you've never
seen a miracle, look closer. They are happening
all around you.

TODAY'S PLAN

*How might it change your prayers to know that God is able
and willing to perform miracles for you?*

ENDURANCE

TODAY'S PROMISE

You know that when your faith is tested, your endurance has a chance to grow. So let it grow, for when your endurance is fully developed, you will be perfect and complete, needing nothing. —JAMES 1:3-4

TODAY'S THOUGHT

Endurance in your faith produces all kinds of good character traits. Endurance is like the fire that purifies precious metals and hardens valuable pottery. It cleanses, clarifies, and solidifies your faith. Living through the trials and tests of life is often the most significant way to discover the riches of your faith and develop godly character.

TODAY'S PLAN

In what ways is your faith being tested? What character traits are being refined?

SPIRITUAL GIFTS

TODAY'S PROMISE

There are different kinds of spiritual gifts, but the same Spirit is the source of them all. There are different kinds of service, but we serve the same Lord. God works in different ways, but it is the same God who does the work in all of us. A spiritual gift is given to each of us so we can help each other.

—1 CORINTHIANS 12:4-7

TODAY'S THOUGHT

The natural abilities you have are gifts from God, and they are often a clue to God's purpose for you. You may have abilities in the areas of cooking, handling money, playing an instrument, or working with children. Use whatever gifts God has given you to bring honor and glory to him. Then you will be right where you need to be to discover God's will for you and to fulfill the purpose for which he created you.

TODAY'S PLAN

How has God called you to serve him with your gifts in this coming year?

HAPPINESS

TODAY'S PROMISE

I know the LORD is always with me. . . . He is right beside me. No wonder my heart is glad, and I rejoice.
—PSALM 16:8-9

TODAY'S THOUGHT

Is happiness merely a passing emotion or a permanent state? The Bible says it can be both. There is happiness that reacts to events (this is temporary and volatile), and there is happiness that overrules circumstances (which is strong and lasting). Happiness based on events is part of life, but if that is all you can count on, you have to keep feeding yourself with new situations to stay upbeat. Those who know the joy that comes from God don't need events to keep them happy. They experience true joy because they know that no matter what happens, God is with them and offers hope and promise.

TODAY'S PLAN

Are you looking for happiness or for true and lasting joy?

CALL OF GOD

TODAY'S PROMISE

Now may the God of peace—who brought up from the dead our Lord Jesus . . . equip you with all you need for doing his will. May he produce in you, through the power of Jesus Christ, every good thing that is pleasing to him. —HEBREWS 13:20-21

TODAY'S THOUGHT

When God calls, he equips. He may have called you to a certain career, or to raise a family, or to a particular ministry in the church or community. Whatever the call, he will give you what you need to fulfill it. Commit yourself to answering his call, and you can be sure he will equip you with the heart, vision, support, and resources you need to carry it out.

TODAY'S PLAN

What resources do you think God has given you to respond to his call?

ENTHUSIASM

TODAY'S PROMISE

I will be filled with joy because of you. I will sing praises to your name, O Most High. —PSALM 9:2

TODAY'S THOUGHT

There are areas of the Christian life that are very serious—sin and its consequences, church discipline, fighting the presence of evil. But there is also great joy in knowing that the God of the universe loves you, has a plan for you, and made this wonderful world for you. In fact, he tells you to serve him enthusiastically, joyfully, and with a great sense of delight. God understands that enthusiasm lights the fire of service.

TODAY'S PLAN

What is it about your faith that gives you joy? How can you let others see that joy more clearly?

SEPTEMBER

SPIRITUAL DRYNESS

TODAY'S PROMISE

The LORD will guide you continually, giving you water when you are dry and restoring your strength. You will be like a well-watered garden, like an ever-flowing spring.

—ISAIAH 58:11

TODAY'S THOUGHT

We can all relate to that parched feeling where we long for a cup of cold water. Your soul can become dry too, thirsting for something that will be truly fulfilling. Seasons of spiritual drought can come when you experience the blazing pressures of the world or the heat of temptation. Just as God sends the rains to refresh the earth, he also sends opportunities to revive your passion and purpose for him. When you see the chance to refresh your soul, act immediately, before the dryness in it causes unnecessary damage to your faith.

TODAY'S PLAN

Are you thirsting for God?

THOUGHTS

TODAY'S PROMISE

Fix your thoughts on what is true, and honorable, and right, and pure, and lovely, and admirable. Think about things that are excellent and worthy of praise. . . . Then the God of peace will be with you.

—PHILIPPIANS 4:8-9

TODAY'S THOUGHT

What you think about reveals what you're really like on the inside. In other words, the quality of your thoughts is an important measure of the condition of your heart. If you are consistently grateful for what you have, those thoughts of gratitude come from a grateful heart. If you are constantly complaining about your circumstances, the negative thoughts are coming from an ungrateful heart. When you focus on thankfulness, praise, love, and joy, your thoughts will soon follow.

TODAY'S PLAN

What do you spend time thinking about that you wish you didn't? How can God help you change your thought life?

COMMUNITY

TODAY'S PROMISE

He makes the whole body fit together perfectly. As each part does its own special work, it helps the other parts grow, so that the whole body is healthy and growing and full of love.
—EPHESIANS 4:16

TODAY'S THOUGHT

People were created for community. Jesus commissioned the church to be a body of believers, not a collection of individuals. Being connected to other people in loving relationships is important to a life filled with purpose and hope. When you are connected to a community of believers, you have a place to worship together, to support one another, and to have fellowship that can keep you walking steadily on God's path, even during the most difficult times.

TODAY'S PLAN

How closely connected are you to a community of believers?

UNITY

TODAY'S PROMISE

Our bodies have many parts, and God has put each part just where he wants it. How strange a body would be if it had only one part! Yes, there are many parts, but only one body. —1 CORINTHIANS 12:18-20

TODAY'S THOUGHT

The Bible holds unity up as one of the highest goals of Christian relationships—whether in marriages, families, communities, work, or church. The sounds of an orchestra are transformed from cacophony to symphony when the musicians follow the composer's score and the conductor's baton. When believers follow God's plan for their lives and rely on the Holy Spirit to lead them, great diversity within the church can turn into great unity as everyone joins together in service to God.

TODAY'S PLAN

What can you do this week to promote greater unity among those you live and serve with?

ENCOURAGEMENT

TODAY'S PROMISE

Don't use foul or abusive language. Let everything you say be good and helpful, so that your words will be an encouragement to those who hear them.

—EPHESIANS 4:29

TODAY'S THOUGHT

Encouragers help us regain commitment, resolve, and motivation. They inspire us with courage and hope. They help us love and live again. Encouragers bring a beautiful gift, often a spiritual gift, when they offer renewal through encouragement. God promises that when you encourage others, you will give them a divine blessing and be blessed yourself.

TODAY'S PLAN

How can you be an encourager today? Try to find something encouraging and helpful to say to whomever God puts in your path.

BELONGING

TODAY'S PROMISE

Just as our bodies have many parts and each part has a special function, so it is with Christ's body. We are many parts of one body, and we all belong to each other. In his grace, God has given us different gifts for doing certain things well. —ROMANS 12:4-6

TODAY'S THOUGHT

The church is called Christ's body because it is made up of Christians who are all different and have different roles to play in his work. If you are a Christian, you are part of Christ's body. Each member of Christ's body is given different abilities and skills so that everyone has important work to do. God promises that you have what it takes to make a difference in the church and in the world. Your fellow believers don't just want you there. They need you!

TODAY'S PLAN

No one wants to be alone. How can I know I belong in fellowship with God's people?

GENTLENESS

TODAY'S PROMISE

He will feed his flock like a shepherd. He will carry the lambs in his arms, holding them close to his heart. He will gently lead the mother sheep with their young.

—ISAIAH 40:11

TODAY'S THOUGHT

In a world full of violence, the concept of gentleness is most welcome. The peace in the hearts of those who are gentle soothes the hearts of others. Jesus was gentle, but that didn't rob him of authority, because gentleness is power under control. The Bible calls us to be gentle in our dealings with others, not only because it is kind and right, but also because it promotes peace.

TODAY'S PLAN

How can you work on being more gentle?

WILL OF GOD

TODAY'S PROMISE

*O LORD, you have examined my heart and know
everything about me. You know when I sit down or
stand up. You know my thoughts even when I'm far
away. . . . You know what I am going to say even
before I say it, LORD. You go before me and follow
me. You place your hand of blessing on my head.*

—PSALM 139:1-2, 4-5

TODAY'S THOUGHT

As you wait to see what God wants you to do
specifically, his will first and foremost is that
you live obediently. When you are ushered into
eternity, which will matter more: what house, car,
or job you had—or what kind of heart you had?
The issue will be whether you have been faithful, loved others, and come to know God in
a special way. God is vitally interested in the
details of your life, but his primary will for all
people is simple obedience.

TODAY'S PLAN

What act of simple obedience can you do today?

FAITHFULNESS

TODAY'S PROMISE

Praise the LORD! How joyful are those who fear the LORD and delight in obeying his commands. Their children will be successful everywhere; an entire generation of godly people will be blessed . . . and their good deeds will last forever. —PSALM 112:1-3

TODAY'S THOUGHT

The Lord blesses those who try to be faithful. And typical of him, he causes his blessings to overflow beyond you to others. As you walk faithfully with God, his blessings will extend to those you live and serve with, because a person passionate for God can make an enormous impact.

TODAY'S PLAN

Is your faithfulness to God rubbing off on others? If so, thank God for this blessing.

OVERWHELMED

TODAY'S PROMISE

When I am overwhelmed, you alone know the way I should turn.
—PSALM 142:3

TODAY'S THOUGHT

When you feel overwhelmed, it can either produce frantic activity or cause you to give up in despair. When it feels as if life is becoming too much to handle, take some time, even if it's just a few minutes, to consult the One who knows the path ahead. Ask him to help you take the first step in the right direction. He knows how to guide you through the most overwhelming of situations.

TODAY'S PLAN

What overwhelming situations are you facing right now? Have you asked God to direct you through them?

COPING

TODAY'S PROMISE

When you go through deep waters, I will be with you. When you go through rivers of difficulty, you will not drown. When you walk through the fire of oppression, you will not be burned up; the flames will not consume you.
—ISAIAH 43:2

TODAY'S THOUGHT

God doesn't promise to save you from trouble. In fact, this verse says, "When you go through deep waters." It assumes that adversity will come your way. But God promises to be with you in your troubles, to give you wisdom to cope, strength to overcome, and understanding about how you can be stronger as you learn to deal with and overcome your problems.

TODAY'S PLAN

Are you asking God the wrong question? Do you ask him to get you out of your problems or to help you become stronger through them?

FRIENDS

TODAY'S PROMISE

If we are living in the light, as God is in the light, then we have fellowship with each other, and the blood of Jesus, his Son, cleanses us from all sin.

—1 JOHN 1:7

TODAY'S THOUGHT

Good friends are a wonderful gift. Fellowship among believers in Jesus (at church or in small groups) is unique because it invites the living God into your midst. Christian fellowship provides a place to share the things in life that really matter, encouragement to stay strong in the face of temptation and persecution, and supernatural help in dealing with difficulties. Bring more of Jesus into your circle of friends, and watch how his light shines through each of you and empowers you to experience the kind of fellowship God created friends for.

TODAY'S PLAN

How much of Jesus do you bring into your friendships?

ABILITIES

TODAY'S PROMISE

In his grace, God has given us different gifts for doing certain things well. —ROMANS 12:6

TODAY'S THOUGHT

God has given every person some special abilities; he leaves no one empty-handed. When you feel as if you have nothing to offer, remember that God has built into you a set of gifts and abilities "for doing certain things well." You certainly do have something to offer!

TODAY'S PLAN

Have you discovered your special God-given abilities? If not, can you commit to doing so?

STRESS

TODAY'S PROMISE

I will call to you whenever I'm in trouble, and you will answer me.
—PSALM 86:7

TODAY'S THOUGHT

Stress puts great pressure on your health and relationships. It is a warning sign that you are being stretched to your limit. But stress can be positive if you learn and grow from it. Just as a muscle can grow only under stress, God promises that your wisdom and character will grow under the pressures of life. As you look for what God is teaching you in your stressful times, you will become better equipped to deal with stressful situations in the future.

TODAY'S PLAN

How can you recognize the positive growth that is coming from your stress?

HEALING

TODAY'S PROMISE

Moved with compassion, Jesus reached out and touched him. "I am willing," he said. "Be healed!" Instantly the leprosy disappeared, and the man wa healed.
                                                    —MARK 1:41-42

TODAY'S THOUGHT

When Jesus touched the leper, he revealed both God's power and compassion for the whole person. God can and does heal today—through the body's natural processes, through medical science, and through miraculous means. But the greatest disease is sin, which disfigures the soul. Although there are no guarantees that Jesus will heal your physical sicknesses in this life, he absolutely promises to heal the disease of sin in anyone who asks.

TODAY'S PLAN

Has Jesus healed the part of you that is sick with sin?

WORRY

TODAY'S PROMISE

[Jesus said,] "Don't let your hearts be troubled. Trust in God, and trust also in me." —JOHN 14:1

Give all your worries and cares to God, for he cares about you. —1 PETER 5:7

TODAY'S THOUGHT

When you are overwhelmed with problems and the worry that comes along with them, don't let discouragement become so strong that you no longer think God cares or wants to help you. Never stop believing that God cares deeply about you. If you give up on God, you will cut off your greatest source of help. Instead, give your worries *to* God, and watch how he helps you.

TODAY'S PLAN

What areas of worry are you having difficulty giving up to God?

BUSYNESS

TODAY'S PROMISE

He lets me rest in green meadows; he leads me beside peaceful streams. —PSALM 23:2

TODAY'S THOUGHT

Activity itself is not a virtue; it can sometimes be a detriment to your spiritual life. It is important to plan time in your busy schedule for rest and renewal. If you are not proactive about this, the other demands of life will completely dictate your schedule. God planned for work, but he also planned for rest, and he invites you to rest and be refreshed in his care. When you follow his prescription for rest, you will find peace.

TODAY'S PLAN

In what way has God prescribed rest for you?

CONFIDENCE

TODAY'S PROMISE

Dear friends, we are already God's children, but he has not yet shown us what we will be like when Christ appears. But we do know that we will be like him.

—1 JOHN 3:2

TODAY'S THOUGHT

Healthy confidence is a realization that you are made to be like Christ. This gives you the assurance that God loves you. He has given you talents and gifts that come from the very character of God, and he wants you to use those gifts for him. He has also given you the gift of salvation and eternal life in heaven. Knowing this gives you complete certainty that your life can have meaning now and forever.

TODAY'S PLAN

How can knowing you have many of God's qualities give you greater confidence as you interact with others today?

FAITH

TODAY'S PROMISE

[Jesus] said, "I tell you the truth, unless you turn from your sins and become like little children, you will never get into the Kingdom of Heaven. So anyone who becomes as humble as this little child is the greatest in the Kingdom of Heaven.

—MATTHEW 18:3-4

TODAY'S THOUGHT

Children demonstrate the kind of innocence, curiosity, and faith that is so dear to God. They approach life wanting to experience new adventures and learn about the world around them, and they trust their parents to be there to guide and comfort. God wants all his children to approach life the same way. He is delighted when we are willing to follow him on the adventure of life, learn all we can about him, and rely on him for guidance and comfort.

TODAY'S PLAN

Are you enjoying the adventure of faith and trusting God as a child would?

STABILITY

TODAY'S PROMISE

The LORD's plans stand firm forever; his intentions can never be shaken. —PSALM 33:11

Teach me to do your will, for you are my God. May your gracious Spirit lead me forward on a firm footing. —PSALM 143:10

TODAY'S THOUGHT

Stability is a state of the heart and mind, not a lifestyle that is conditional on so many tentative factors. It comes from a consistently growing relationship with God. Stability is not determined by the circumstances around you, which you cannot predict and which always change. Stability is determined by the changeless principles and promises of God, which allow you to respond to any circumstance with strong faith and confidence.

TODAY'S PLAN

How do you respond to difficult circumstances?

HABITS

TODAY'S PROMISE

Those who are dominated by the sinful nature think about sinful things, but those who are controlled by the Holy Spirit think about things that please the Spirit. So letting your sinful nature control your mind leads to death. But letting the Spirit control your mind leads to life and peace.

—ROMANS 8:5-6

TODAY'S THOUGHT

The sinful nature you inherited at birth is very powerful. It will dominate your thinking unless you have a greater power to defeat it. If you've dedicated your life to Jesus, he has placed the Holy Spirit inside you. You are not strong enough to fight your sinful nature, but the Holy Spirit is. Let him control your heart and mind, and you will begin to get rid of not just your bad habits but your sinful ones as well.

TODAY'S PLAN

What are some habits you're trying to break all by yourself? Have you asked for the Holy Spirit's help?

DISCIPLE

TODAY'S PROMISE

[Jesus said,] "My sheep listen to my voice; I know them, and they follow me." —JOHN 10:27

TODAY'S THOUGHT

Being a disciple of Jesus is simply a matter of following him with a willing heart. He will bless you, not because of your ability but because of your availability.

TODAY'S PLAN

How much do you really want to follow Jesus?

GRACE

TODAY'S PROMISE

The wages of sin is death, but the free gift of God is eternal life through Christ Jesus our Lord.

—ROMANS 6:23

TODAY'S THOUGHT

Grace is undeserved favor. The Bible explains how God has extended grace to everyone by offering salvation—eternal life with him—for free! You don't have to do anything to earn it. In fact, you can't. You simply accept it by believing that Jesus, God's Son, died for your sins so that you don't have to. God's ultimate act of grace is an example of how you are to extend grace to others.

TODAY'S PLAN

Who can you give the gift of grace to today?

MISTAKES

TODAY'S PROMISE

He has removed our sins as far from us as the east is from the west. —PSALM 103:12

TODAY'S THOUGHT

There can be a big difference between making a mistake and committing a sin. A mistake is accidentally saying something hurtful. A sin is gossiping or slandering someone. You can often avoid repeating a mistake by studying harder, planning better, or double-checking your work. But to avoid repeating the same sin, you need God's help. The regret you feel over a sin indicates that you want to be different, and God promises that when you confess your sin to him, he will make you different by removing your sin and completely cleaning you on the inside.

TODAY'S PLAN

Have you asked God to make you clean on the inside?

BALANCE

TODAY'S PROMISE

I brought glory to you here on earth by completing the work you gave me to do. Now, Father, bring me into the glory we shared before the world began.

—JOHN 17:4-5

TODAY'S THOUGHT

Jesus came as a living promise that it is possible to live a life of balance. Balance means living a life that honors God, others, and yourself in the way you use your gifts and spend your time and resources. You can easily get out of balance by overemphasizing one set of responsibilities at the cost of others. God assures you that there is time for everything he calls you to do. Jesus, with all of his potential and all the needs around him, left much undone, and yet he accomplished everything God had given him to do.

TODAY'S PLAN

What can be left undone that would be okay with God?

LIMITATIONS

TODAY'S PROMISE

Now all glory to God, who is able, through his mighty power at work within us, to accomplish infinitely more than we might ask or think.

—EPHESIANS 3:20

TODAY'S THOUGHT

God calls out the best in you. He sees more in you than you see in yourself. You may look at your limitations; God looks at your potential. If you want to increase your possibilities, learn to see life from God's perspective. He doesn't put nearly as many limitations on you as you do. He sees you for what he intended you to be and what he created you to do. How encouraging that the God of the universe looks at you for what you can become rather than for what you are.

TODAY'S PLAN

In what areas is God asking more from you?

EXAMPLE

TODAY'S PROMISE

Take a new grip with your tired hands and strengthen your weak knees. Mark out a straight path for your feet so that those who are weak and lame will not fall but become strong.
                                                    —HEBREWS 12:12-13

TODAY'S THOUGHT

Every person on earth is a role model of something to someone. You follow others' examples, and you set an example for others. Your words and actions influence others not only in matters of daily living but also for good or evil, Christ or Satan. What kind of example have you been demonstrating lately to others?

TODAY'S PLAN

How can your words and actions help others want to be more like God?

CALL OF GOD

TODAY'S PROMISE

I knew you before I formed you in your mother's womb. Before you were born I set you apart and appointed you.
                                                    —JEREMIAH 1:5

TODAY'S THOUGHT

Before you were even born, God decided what spiritual gifts and abilities he would give you and how he wanted you to use them. If you don't use the gifts God has given you to fulfill the purpose for which he created you, you are missing out on the best possible life he planned for you. As long as you have life and breath, you can begin to use your God-given gifts and answer your God-given call. It's not too late.

TODAY'S PLAN

Are you asking God to make his call clear to you?

PAIN-FREE

TODAY'S PROMISE

He will swallow up death forever! The Sovereign LORD will wipe away all tears. —ISAIAH 25:8

Our present troubles are small and won't last very long. Yet they produce for us a glory that vastly outweighs them and will last forever!

—2 CORINTHIANS 4:17

TODAY'S THOUGHT

God does not promise believers a life free from pain and suffering. If Christians didn't hurt, other people would see God only as a magician who takes away pain. But as a Christian, you have a relationship with God, who helps you through your hurts, comforts you in your pain, and sometimes miraculously heals your wounds. Whatever pain you are experiencing is temporary; it will end, perhaps here on earth, but certainly in heaven.

TODAY'S PLAN

How might your present hurts be turned into eternal joy?

FORGIVENESS

TODAY'S PROMISE

Make allowance for each other's faults, and forgive anyone who offends you. Remember, the Lord forgave you, so you must forgive others. —COLOSSIANS 3:13

God, with undeserved kindness, declares that we are righteous. He did this through Christ Jesus when he freed us from the penalty for our sins.

—ROMANS 3:24

TODAY'S THOUGHT

Forgiveness is not an option; it is a command. It is necessary for your own health and your relationship with God. Forgiveness doesn't mean that the hurt doesn't exist or that it doesn't matter; nor does it make everything "all right." Forgiveness allows you to let go of the hurt and let God deal with the one who hurt you. Forgiveness sets you free to move on with your life. It's not always easy, but forgiving those who have hurt you is the healthiest thing you can do for yourself.

TODAY'S PLAN

Who do you need to forgive to set you free?

OCTOBER

GENEROSITY

TODAY'S PROMISE

Don't forget to do good and to share with those in need. These are the sacrifices that please God.

—HEBREWS 13:16

TODAY'S THOUGHT

Generosity is both a spiritual gift and a spiritual discipline. Generosity is important to God because it is the opposite of selfishness, one of the most destructive sins. Selfishness promotes greed, stinginess, envy, and hard-heartedness—all traits that destroy relationships. Generosity promotes giving, trust, mercy, and putting the needs of others above your own—all traits that build relationships.

TODAY'S PLAN

How generous are you?

MOTIVES

TODAY'S PROMISE

The LORD's light penetrates the human spirit, exposing every hidden motive. —PROVERBS 20:27

TODAY'S THOUGHT

One person may give a thousand dollars to charity in order to earn a tax break; another may do it to win political favor; still another may act out of deep compassion for the poor. The same act can be set in motion by very different motives. The Bible teaches that God is as interested in your motives as in your behavior, because eventually selfish and sinful motives produce selfish and sinful behavior.

TODAY'S PLAN

Keep honest track of each of your decisions today. How many were based on good motives rather than selfish ones?

BURDENS

TODAY'S PROMISE

*Give your burdens to the LORD, and he will take
care of you.*
—PSALM 55:22

TODAY'S THOUGHT

When your own problems and obstacles consume
you, you give in to fear—that you will fail, that you
will let others down, and that God will not help
you when you most need him. Fear will tempt
you to focus on the size of your burden rather
than on the size of your God. When you focus
on God instead, you will see him fighting by
your side. This kind of faith in God is the only
way to maintain joy and peace in spite of your
circumstances.

TODAY'S PLAN

*Can you honestly say you are giving your burdens over
to God?*

HURTS/HURTING

TODAY'S PROMISE

When you are praying, first forgive anyone you are holding a grudge against, so that your Father in heaven will forgive your sins, too. —MARK 11:25

TODAY'S THOUGHT

Holding grudges against those who have hurt you can actually hinder your relationship with God. When you forgive others, your forgiveness opens your heart to receive God's forgiveness when you sin.

TODAY'S PLAN

What are some grudges that you might be holding in your heart? How are these hurts hindering your relationship with God?

ADVICE

TODAY'S PROMISE

The godly offer good counsel; they teach right from wrong. They have made God's law their own, so they will never slip from his path. —PSALM 37:30-31

TODAY'S THOUGHT

God is wisdom, and he teaches wisdom through his Word. Committing God's Word to heart makes God's wisdom available to you at all times so that you can refer to it when you need to provide or receive advice. Not only will God's Word advise and steady you in your own life, but your words also will be wise and helpful to others.

TODAY'S PLAN

How often do you tap into God's Word when you need advice?

FEAR OF GOD

TODAY'S PROMISE

Fear of the LORD is the foundation of true wisdom. All who obey his commandments will grow in wisdom. Praise him forever! —PSALM 111:10

TODAY'S THOUGHT

To fear the Lord is to recognize that he is holy, mighty, righteous, all-knowing, and wise. When you regard God correctly, you gain a clearer picture of yourself as sinful, weak, and needy. The only response to a God who loves you as you are is to fall at his feet in awe. It is this attitude of humility and reverence that prepares your heart to obey his words and receive the wisdom of his ways.

TODAY'S PLAN

Do you want real wisdom? Have you begun your search by humbly acknowledging God as the source of wisdom?

SPIRITUAL WARFARE

TODAY'S PROMISE

We are not fighting against flesh-and-blood enemies, but against evil rulers and authorities of the unseen world, against mighty powers in this dark world, and against evil spirits in the heavenly places. Therefore, put on every piece of God's armor so you will be able to resist the enemy in the time of evil.

—EPHESIANS 6:12-13

TODAY'S THOUGHT

You are in a spiritual battle with Satan and his evil forces. Determined to destroy your faith, Satan launches surprise attacks with blatant temptation and lies. But God promises to supply you with spiritual weapons to fight back. If you learn how to use them you will not be defeated.

TODAY'S PLAN

Are you adequately trained for life's spiritual battles?

CHARACTER

TODAY'S PROMISE

You are a holy people, who belong to the LORD your God. Of all the people on earth, [he] has chosen you to be his own special treasure.

—DEUTERONOMY 7:6

TODAY'S THOUGHT

Although God was speaking to the Israelites when he gave this promise, it also applies in a general sense to anyone who claims allegiance to him. Those who are called God's people are special—holy, uniquely blessed, and chosen for an important work. Think of it—the God of the universe has chosen you and called you to be his. This is a special privilege but also a special responsibility, because it requires that you live so that you model the very character of God.

TODAY'S PLAN

Is your character growing to match God's call to you?

INTEGRITY

TODAY'S PROMISE

The LORD rewarded me for doing right. He has seen my innocence. To the faithful you show yourself faithful; to those with integrity you show integrity.

—PSALM 18:24-25

TODAY'S THOUGHT

Integrity allows you to continue uninterrupted fellowship with God and helps you live under his spiritual protection and guidance. When you lack integrity, you are exposed to all kinds of sin and danger you wouldn't normally face, including the disintegration of your character.

TODAY'S PLAN

How is your integrity affecting your fellowship with God?

RESPONSIBILITY

TODAY'S PROMISE

To those who use well what they are given, even more will be given, and they will have an abundance. But from those who do nothing, even what little they have will be taken away. —MATTHEW 25:29

TODAY'S THOUGHT

Often it seems that people no longer want to take responsibility for their actions; it's *never* their fault. But God promises that if you take responsibility for your actions, and use what he has given you well, he will give you more opportunities and more blessings. In the end, each person is accountable to God for his or her own decisions, behavior, and relationships. So use well whatever gifts and opportunities God has given you, and he will reward you.

TODAY'S PLAN

What God-given responsibilities do you have?

DISCERNMENT

TODAY'S PROMISE

The gatekeeper opens the gate for him, and the sheep recognize his voice and come to him. He calls his own sheep by name and leads them out. After he has gathered his own flock, he walks ahead of them, and they follow him because they know his voice. They won't follow a stranger; they will run from him because they don't know his voice. —JOHN 10:3-5

TODAY'S THOUGHT

When you really know someone, you can instantly recognize his or her voice. You can pick it out in a crowd. As you spend time studying the teachings of Jesus and getting to know him better, you will get to know his voice. When a person is preaching or teaching, you will be able to tell if what he or she is saying is consistent with what Jesus would say, and you won't be deceived.

TODAY'S PLAN

How well would you say you can recognize the voice of Jesus?

TITHING

TODAY'S PROMISE

[God said,] "Bring all the tithes into the storehouse so there will be enough food in my Temple. If you do," says the LORD of Heaven's Armies, "I will open the windows of heaven for you. I will pour out a blessing so great you won't have enough room to take it in! Try it! Put me to the test!"
—MALACHI 3:10

TODAY'S THOUGHT

When you tithe, you show your commitment to God and his work, honor him for his provision and faithfulness, and help those in need. Regular tithing keeps God at the top of your priority list. Instead of asking, "How much of my money do I need to give to God?" ask yourself, "How much of God's money do I need to keep?" As you fulfill his command to meet others' needs, he graciously meets—and exceeds—your own.

TODAY'S PLAN

How can you develop the discipline of tithing?

APPEARANCE

TODAY'S PROMISE

When they arrived, Samuel took one look at Eliab and thought, "Surely this is the LORD's anointed!" But the LORD said to Samuel, "Don't judge by his appearance or height, for I have rejected him. The LORD doesn't see things the way you see them. People judge by outward appearance, but the LORD looks at the heart." —1 SAMUEL 16:6-7

TODAY'S THOUGHT

The condition of your body does not reveal the condition of your heart. But it doesn't take long for your true colors to show through your outward appearance. The beauty inside always shines brighter than your external looks.

TODAY'S PLAN

Is your appearance deceiving to others?

WORK

Let your good deeds shine out for all to see, so that everyone will praise your heavenly Father.

—MATTHEW 5:16

TODAY'S THOUGHT

You don't need to accomplish earthshaking tasks in order for your work to be meaningful. Your life has meaning when you do the work that God has given you to do. Whether you are changing diapers, running a company, cleaning houses, or serving in a church, your work has meaning because you are doing it for God and sharing with everyone in your circle of influence.

TODAY'S PLAN

What good work can you do today?

COMPASSION

TODAY'S PROMISE

He will rescue the poor when they cry to him; he will help the oppressed, who have no one to defend them. He feels pity for the weak and the needy . . . for their lives are precious to him. —PSALM 72:12-14

If you help the poor, you are lending to the LORD—and he will repay you! —PROVERBS 19:17

TODAY'S THOUGHT

Personal salvation should bear fruit in social compassion. God expects you to share what he has given you with those in need. The poor, orphans, and widows are symbolic of many who need the loving support of God's people. Helping the poor, lonely, and needy reminds you of how much God helps you when your soul is poor, lonely, and needy. When you help those in need, God will help you more!

TODAY'S PLAN

Who is in need that God has placed in your life? How can you help them?

FAITH

TODAY'S PROMISE

If we are faithful to the end, trusting God just as firmly as when we first believed, we will share in all that belongs to Christ. —HEBREWS 3:14

TODAY'S THOUGHT

Faith in God means that we are willing to trust him with our very lives. We are willing to follow his guidelines for living as outlined in the Bible because we have the conviction that this will be best for us. We are even willing to endure ridicule and persecution for our faith because we are so sure that God is who he says he is and that he will keep his promises about salvation and life forever with him in heaven.

TODAY'S PLAN

Would you say your faith has been growing or shrinking lately? How can you get it to keep growing?

ENCOURAGEMENT

TODAY'S PROMISE

Be strong and courageous! Do not be afraid or discouraged. For the LORD your God is with you wherever you go. —JOSHUA 1:9

The LORD will go ahead of you; yes, the God of Israel will protect you from behind. —ISAIAH 52:12

TODAY'S THOUGHT

Do you ever feel alone or that you are sailing into uncharted waters? Would it encourage you to know that God is with you each step of the way? He promises he is. Even more than that, he has gone before you to prepare the hearts and minds of those you will interact with, and he is still behind you protecting your backside. He is with you, behind you, and ahead of you. Wherever you go, you are encircled by almighty God.

TODAY'S PLAN

Do you need more courage to move into a situation where you believe God is prompting you to go? With God encircling you, what is stopping you?

PASSION

TODAY'S PROMISE

We must listen very carefully to the truth we have heard, or we may drift away from it. —HEBREWS 2:1

TODAY'S THOUGHT

Like all relationships, your relationship with God takes effort and energy. God is fully committed to you. In order for your relationship to continue to be passionate and exciting, you must be fully committed to him—diligent in your efforts to know him better. Consistent study of God's Word, along with a thankful heart and acts of service toward others, will fight off feelings of apathy toward God and renew your focus on his purpose for your life and the blessings he has already given you and wants to give you in the future.

TODAY'S PLAN

Where are you feeling apathetic in your spiritual life? What first step can you take to change that?

CHALLENGES

TODAY'S PROMISE

Commit everything you do to the LORD. Trust him, and he will help you.

—PSALM 37:5

TODAY'S THOUGHT

No detail of your life is too small for God. He is interested in every detail of your life. You are not interrupting him or irritating him when you talk to him about those details. When you commit all your plans to him, he commits himself and his infinite resources to you.

TODAY'S PLAN

Do you feel as if some problems are too small to bring to God? He wants you to feel comfortable talking to him about everything.

PERSEVERANCE

TODAY'S PROMISE

The Sovereign LORD is my strength! He makes me as surefooted as a deer, able to tread upon the heights. —HABAKKUK 3:19

TODAY'S THOUGHT

If you don't learn to persevere through your struggles, you will get into the habit of giving up. But when you persevere until you come out on the other side, you grow stronger in faith, you see the benefits of obedience to God, and you develop greater confidence that when problems strike again, you can get through them.

TODAY'S PLAN

When facing troubles, determine to come out the other side stronger. Have you asked God for the courage to move ahead over the obstacles in your life?

EVIL

TODAY'S PROMISE

Be strong in the Lord and in his mighty power.
Put on all of God's armor so that you will be able to
stand firm against all strategies of the devil.

—EPHESIANS 6:10-11

TODAY'S THOUGHT

Since the fall of humankind, the earth has not
known a time without the influence of evil. We
face an enemy far more powerful than any human
foe. That enemy is Satan, the very embodiment
of evil. His goal is to overcome good with evil,
in your life and in the world. But God has given
us powerful spiritual weapons and armor to fight
against the forces of evil, and he has promised
victory to all those who believe in him.

TODAY'S PLAN

How can you dress yourself with God's spiritual armor
today?

GRIEF

TODAY'S PROMISE

God blesses those who mourn, for they will be comforted. —MATTHEW 5:4

TODAY'S THOUGHT

All people experience some form of grief in times of loss. But those who live in relationship with God through Jesus Christ grieve with hope. You grieve because you experience real pain, but you grieve with hope because you know God can and will redeem your pain into something good. God does not waste your sorrows, because even your pain brings the comfort of Jesus himself.

TODAY'S PLAN

When you are grieving, will you allow God to redeem your pain?

SAFETY

TODAY'S PROMISE

[Christ] never sinned, but he died for sinners to bring you safely home to God. He suffered physical death, but he was raised to life in the Spirit. —1 PETER 3:18

TODAY'S THOUGHT

Although God is concerned about what happens to your body, he is much more concerned about the safety of your soul. Once you have confessed faith in Jesus and the Holy Spirit comes to live in you, he is at work protecting your soul from being snatched away by Satan. This is the essence of God's promise of protection. God is concerned about your safety, and you probably experience his hand of protection much more than you realize.

TODAY'S PLAN

How secure should you feel knowing that your soul is safe for eternity?

APATHY

TODAY'S PROMISE

[Jesus said,] "Anyone who isn't with me opposes me, and anyone who isn't working with me is actually working against me." —MATTHEW 12:30

TODAY'S THOUGHT

Apathy causes you to lose what you want the most. If a woman is apathetic toward her husband, she is in danger of losing him. If you are apathetic toward God, you are in danger of missing out on the priceless rewards that await his followers in heaven. Apathy is not only a passive force that lulls you to sleep; it can also be an aggressive force that works to prevent you from keeping what is most meaningful and important.

TODAY'S PLAN

Are you in danger of losing something dear to you? How might apathy be playing a role?

MONEY

TODAY'S PROMISE

Honor the LORD with your wealth and with the best part of everything you produce. Then he will fill your barns with grain, and your vats will overflow with good wine.

—PROVERBS 3:9–10

TODAY'S THOUGHT

Instead of viewing money as yours to use as you wish, see it as God's, to use as *he* wishes. Giving back to God the first part of everything you receive will help you maintain this perspective, and God promises to bless you for it.

TODAY'S PLAN

Is God your first priority when it comes to money? If not, what can you do to change that?

ENEMIES

TODAY'S PROMISE

Don't repay evil for evil. Don't retaliate with insults when people insult you. Instead, pay them back with a blessing. That is what God has called you to do, and he will bless you for it. —1 PETER 3:9

TODAY'S THOUGHT

An enemy is anyone who tries to hurt you. This verse isn't saying that you should just let someone hurt you. But it does promise that when you respond to your enemies with forgiveness, when you pray for them, and when you don't retaliate, God will bless you for it. This is what sets Christians apart from the rest of the world. It is better to experience the blessing of God than the human satisfaction of revenge.

TODAY'S PLAN

Who are your enemies? How do you bless them?

BODY

TODAY'S PROMISE

Don't you realize that your body is the temple of the Holy Spirit, who lives in you and was given to you by God? You do not belong to yourself, for God bought you with a high price. So you must honor God with your body. —1 CORINTHIANS 6:19-20

TODAY'S THOUGHT

Your body was made to worship and glorify God and to fulfill the purpose for which he created you. When you do things that are destructive to your body, you are breaking down the vessel God wants to use to help accomplish his work in the world. Because God chooses to work through people, he must work through your body, not just your spirit, to get things done. Take care of your body so that you are ready for the great things God wants to do through you.

TODAY'S PLAN

Are you honoring God with your body?

CONFLICT

TODAY'S PROMISE

[Jesus said,] "You have heard the law that says, 'Love your neighbor' and hate your enemy. But I say, love your enemies! Pray for those who persecute you! In that way, you will be acting as true children of your Father in heaven." —MATTHEW 5:43-45

TODAY'S THOUGHT

Human nature wants to love friends and hate enemies. But Jesus brought a new order that adds a divine perspective—the only way to resolve some conflicts is to reach out in love to your enemy. You can know that you are maturing as a child of God when your natural reaction becomes to reach out in love to those who are against you.

TODAY'S PLAN

Who wants to see you fail? How can you show love to that person?

BURNOUT

TODAY'S PROMISE

It is not by force nor by strength, but by my Spirit, says the LORD of Heaven's Armies. —ZECHARIAH 4:6

TODAY'S THOUGHT

Because burnout is so draining and paralyzing, you need to take care of your body and mind by eating right, exercising, and getting adequate sleep and rest. Even more, one of the best ways to reduce burnout is by taking time to be close to God. When you draw close to him, you can tap into his power, strength, peace, protection, and love. Doing this can help you stay strong and persevere through even the worst times of burnout.

TODAY'S PLAN

What steps can you take to draw closer to God?

ESCAPE

TODAY'S PROMISE

The temptations in your life are no different from what others experience. And God is faithful. He will not allow the temptation to be more than you can stand. When you are tempted, he will show you a way out so that you can endure.

—1 CORINTHIANS 10:13

TODAY'S THOUGHT

Don't underestimate the power of Satan, but don't overestimate it either. He can tempt you, but he cannot force you to sin. He can dangle the bait in front of you, but he cannot make you take it. The Bible promises that no temptation will ever be too strong for you to resist. Even in times of heavy temptation, God will provide a way out. In these times of temptation, the Holy Spirit gives you the power and wisdom to find the way of escape.

TODAY'S PLAN

What temptation do you need an escape from?

OPPOSITION

TODAY'S PROMISE

[Jesus said,] "The world would love you as one of its own if you belonged to it, but you are no longer part of the world. I chose you to come out of the world, so it hates you."

—JOHN 15:19

TODAY'S THOUGHT

Evil can't stand the sight of Jesus or bear to hear his name. So if you are living so that others can see Jesus in you, you will face opposition and even persecution for your faith. If you are for Jesus, you and he share a common enemy in Satan. But with Jesus on your side, you cannot lose the battle for your soul. Even if the whole world is against you, God promises spiritual victories in this life, and ultimate victory for eternity.

TODAY'S PLAN

In what area are you experiencing spiritual opposition?

NOVEMBER

BLESSINGS

TODAY'S PROMISE

How joyful are those who fear the LORD—all who follow his ways! —PSALM 128:1

TODAY'S THOUGHT

Throughout the Bible, you find a simple but profound principle: Obeying God brings blessing, and disobeying God brings misfortune. But be careful not to think of these blessings in terms only of material possessions. The greatest blessings are far more valuable than money or possessions. They come in the form of joy, family, relationships, a well-functioning home, peace of mind, spiritual gifts, and the confidence of eternal life. A life focused on God brings joy to God and many blessings to you. The more you trust and obey God, the more you will experience the blessings he gives.

TODAY'S PLAN

Other than happiness, what are some other blessings you experience through obeying God? In what ways can you pursue those blessings today?

FAMILY

TODAY'S PROMISE

"This is my covenant with them," says the LORD. "My Spirit will not leave them, and neither will these words I have given you. They will be on your lips and on the lips of your children and your children's children forever." —ISAIAH 59:21

TODAY'S THOUGHT

Too often we think in individualistic terms. But God cares about groups of people too, especially families, because a group of people passionate about God can make an enormous impact. So pray not just for the individuals in your family, but for your family as a whole, that God will use you collectively to accomplish good things for him.

TODAY'S PLAN

What can your family do together to serve God?

VISION

TODAY'S PROMISE

The people's minds were hardened, and to this day whenever the old covenant is being read, the same veil covers their minds so they cannot understand the truth. And this veil can be removed only by believing in Christ. —2 CORINTHIANS 3:14

TODAY'S THOUGHT

It seems ironic that for many of us the only way to see clearly is to cover our eyes with glass lenses. With spiritual vision, you need the lens of faith—the ability to believe that there is much more happening than you can see. When you face difficulties that seem insurmountable, remember that spiritual armies are fighting for your soul. Open your spiritual eyes to view God's power.

TODAY'S PLAN

How can you develop better spiritual eyesight?

GENEROSITY

TODAY'S PROMISE

You must each decide in your heart how much to give. And don't give reluctantly or in response to pressure. "For God loves a person who gives cheerfully." And God will generously provide all you need. Then you will always have everything you need and plenty left over to share with others.

—2 CORINTHIANS 9:7-8

TODAY'S THOUGHT

God looks more at the willing heart than at the amount. God looks for what giving will do in your life, not just what it will accomplish for his Kingdom. Does your giving sometimes cause you to do without something important to you? Can you honestly say you give sacrificially? That kind of giving reveals true generosity. That is the giving God rewards.

TODAY'S PLAN

How could you give more willingly and sacrificially?

WORD OF GOD

TODAY'S PROMISE

The instructions of the LORD are perfect, reviving the soul. The decrees of the LORD are trustworthy, making wise the simple. The commandments of the LORD are right, bringing joy to the heart. The commands of the LORD are clear, giving insight for living.
—PSALM 19:7-8

TODAY'S THOUGHT

Reading God's Word every day keeps you in the presence of the One who created you, who knows you best, and who can guide you along the best pathway for your life. If you open your heart to the words recorded in the Bible, you will begin to experience comfort, joy, insight, wisdom, knowledge, and the keys to living. You can always experience God, just by reading his Word!

TODAY'S PLAN

When you open your Bible, do you expect to experience the presence of God?

NEIGHBORS

TODAY'S PROMISE

A second [commandment] is equally important: "Love your neighbor as yourself." —MATTHEW 22:39

If you love your neighbor, you will fulfill the requirements of God's law. —ROMANS 13:8

TODAY'S THOUGHT

Jesus said that loving your neighbor as yourself is the second-greatest commandment. God knows that your first instinct is to take care of yourself. If you can train yourself to give the needs of others equal priority with your own, then you will have learned what love is really about. Love directed inward has nowhere else to go. Love directed outward can change the world, one person at a time.

TODAY'S PLAN

How well are you doing at loving your neighbors?

CONSEQUENCES

TODAY'S PROMISE

Those who live only to satisfy their own sinful nature will harvest decay and death from that sinful nature. But those who live to please the Spirit will harvest everlasting life from the Spirit. —GALATIANS 6:8

TODAY'S THOUGHT

Satan often tempts you to sin with the thought, *It won't hurt anybody.* But sin always hurts someone and destroys something. When temptation comes, remember that it is often beautifully wrapped around a lie. Sin always has negative consequences, but the reverse is also true: Living to please God always has positive consequences.

TODAY'S PLAN

Have you allowed yourself to believe Satan's lie that a little sin won't hurt anybody? How can you unwrap his disguise so you can see the ugly consequences of your actions before you go ahead with them?

TEAMWORK

All of you together are Christ's body, and each of you is a part of it. —1 CORINTHIANS 12:27

The large body of an airplane, made of thousands of complex, moving parts seems to fly effortlessly in the sky while carrying hundreds of people, monitoring hundreds of different systems, and knowing exactly where it's going. Christians should be like that plane. We are part of a larger body of believers (a family, a church, an organization, a missions team). Each person is an important piece of Christ's body. God promises that when we are all in our correct place and working with others as we should be, we bring God's message to new heights and carry many others with us.

How can you develop and encourage a spirit of teamwork with other Christians around you?

PATIENCE

TODAY'S PROMISE

The Holy Spirit produces this kind of fruit in our lives: . . . patience.   —GALATIANS 5:22

TODAY'S THOUGHT

If you've ever spent hours stuck in rush-hour traffic or held a crying baby at 2:00 a.m., you know something about patience. According to the Bible, patience is a form of perseverance and endurance that allows you to respond to frustrating circumstances with grace and self-control. Patience is not merely a personality trait. It is a by-product of the presence and work of the Holy Spirit in the hearts and minds of believers. The greater the presence of the Holy Spirit in you, the more patience you will have.

TODAY'S PLAN

How can you allow the Holy Spirit to develop greater patience in your life?

DOUBT

TODAY'S PROMISE

He has given us great and precious promises. These are the promises that enable you to share his divine nature and escape the world's corruption caused by human desires. In view of all this, make every effort to respond to God's promises. —2 PETER 1:4-5

TODAY'S THOUGHT

God promises to continue to renew your hope and faith. Search God's Word for his great promises, and patiently watch for their fulfillment. Let God answer your questions, but trust him to answer on his schedule, not yours. Don't throw away your faith just because God doesn't resolve your doubt immediately. Enduring through times of doubt and discouragement will make you stronger and more confident in your relationship with God and in God's ultimate promise of eternal life.

TODAY'S PLAN

How can your doubts actually increase your confidence in God?

FREEDOM

TODAY'S PROMISE

We give great honor to those who endure under suffering.

—JAMES 5:11

TODAY'S THOUGHT

Every country honors its soldiers who endure much suffering on behalf of its citizens. Soldiers are heroes who are willing to give up their lives so that others might live theirs to the fullest. The Christian faith also has heroes: those who inspire us to hang on to our faith no matter what happens, those who are willing to give up their lives for what they believe. Determine to be faithful to God no matter what, and experience the greatest of freedoms—freedom from eternal death.

TODAY'S PLAN

God may not ask you to be a martyr for him, but is your faith strong enough to endure even a little derision or scorn?

FAITH

TODAY'S PROMISE

Abram believed the LORD, and the LORD counted him as righteous because of his faith. —GENESIS 15:6

[Jesus said] "I am the resurrection and the life. Anyone who believes in me will live, even after dying. Everyone who lives in me and believes in me will never ever die. Do you believe . . . ?"

—JOHN 11:25-26

TODAY'S THOUGHT

Abram made many mistakes, so how could God call him "righteous"? It was faith, not perfection, that made him right in God's eyes. This same principle is true for you. Rather than measuring your goodness, God is looking for your faith and your willingness to follow him. When the Lord finds faith, he declares you righteous.

TODAY'S PLAN

Are you more interested in faith or in trying to be good? Do you really believe?

POOR

TODAY'S PROMISE

Feed the hungry, and help those in trouble. Then your light will shine out from the darkness, and the darkness around you will be as bright as noon.

—ISAIAH 58:10

TODAY'S THOUGHT

God has deep compassion for the poor, so if you want to become more like God, you must also show compassion for the poor. Compassion that does not reach into your checkbook or onto your "to do" list is philosophical compassion, not godly compassion. Helping the poor is not merely an obligation; it is a privilege that not only brings great joy but also brings a reward from God himself.

TODAY'S PLAN

Is there anything you can do today to help someone less fortunate than you?

CHANGE

TODAY'S PROMISE

I am certain that God, who began the good work within you, will continue his work until it is finally finished on the day when Christ Jesus returns.

—PHILIPPIANS 1:6

TODAY'S THOUGHT

A great work takes a long time to complete. Though we become believers in a moment of faith, the process of transformation into Christlikeness takes a lifetime. Although it may appear slow to us, God's work his people is relentless and certain.

TODAY'S PLAN

How is God working to change you?

HERITAGE

TODAY'S PROMISE

When you believed in Christ, he identified you as his own by giving you the Holy Spirit, whom he promised long ago. The Spirit is God's guarantee that he will give us the inheritance he promised.

—EPHESIANS 1:13-14

TODAY'S THOUGHT

You can't choose the heritage you were born into, but you can choose a spiritual heritage that comes from joining the family of God, which has spanned the centuries since the beginning of time. All who claim allegiance to Jesus Christ are God's children, and if you love, obey, and honor him, he promises to start his own spiritual heritage through you. Unlike any other heritage, this one will last for eternity.

TODAY'S PLAN

Are you leaving a spiritual heritage for those who come after you?

SUCCESS

TODAY'S PROMISE

[Jesus said,] "Anyone who listens to my teaching and follows it is wise, like a person who builds a house on solid rock. Though the rain comes in torrents and the floodwaters rise and the winds beat against that house, it won't collapse because it is built on bedrock."

—MATTHEW 7:24-25

TODAY'S THOUGHT

Your sense of failure may be determined by the approval—or lack of approval—of others. Scripture reminds you to define success in terms of faithfulness to God. God will reward your faithfulness even if you "fail" in the eyes of the world, and then your life will rest on a firm foundation that will last forever.

TODAY'S PLAN

What can you do today to be successful in God's eyes?

AGING

TODAY'S PROMISE

I will be your God throughout your lifetime—until your hair is white with age. I made you, and I will care for you. I will carry you along and save you.

—ISAIAH 46:4

TODAY'S THOUGHT

God's love lasts for all your days. This promise gives you a wonderful picture of God's care. He walks alongside you and carries you when you can no longer walk. In the end he will carry you into eternity, bringing you through death to your final, glorious destination, where age will no longer be relevant and you will be strong and vital forever.

TODAY'S PLAN

Can you see aging as God's eternal beautification process?

GUIDANCE

TODAY'S PROMISE

You guide me with your counsel, leading me to a glorious destiny.

—PSALM 73:24

TODAY'S THOUGHT

God knows where you've been, and what will happen in the future. When you seek his advice, he points you to places of unimaginable beauty, joy, and peace and also helps you avoid danger spots. God promises to be your constant guide, leading you through the dark valleys and over the mountaintop experiences and bringing you to that place of eternal peace and rest everyone longs for but cannot find without him.

TODAY'S PLAN

Are you confident that you are following God wherever he is leading you?

DISCIPLINE

TODAY'S PROMISE

Joyful are those you discipline, LORD, those you teach with your instructions. —PSALM 94:12

TODAY'S THOUGHT

No one likes pain, and no one wants to hear that it is "good for you." But the truth is that without discipline, people are prone to do the wrong things and suffer the consequences. Effective discipline sets you back on the right path, making you thankful to be once again going the right way. And who better to discipline you than a perfect and loving God who knows just what you need to do right and to avoid disaster. God promises that when he disciplines you, it is always to improve on who you are and how you live.

TODAY'S PLAN

If God were to discipline you, in what area might he do it? What good can you envision as a result of his discipline?

CELEBRATION

TODAY'S PROMISE

There you and your families will feast in the presence of the LORD your God, and you will rejoice in all you have accomplished because the LORD your God has blessed you.

—DEUTERONOMY 12:7

TODAY'S THOUGHT

Celebrations are an effective way to bond family members to each other and to God. By celebrating together, you are creating memories of faithfulness to God and to each other, which will later bring great joy and praise to God for giving you such blessings.

TODAY'S PLAN

What are some family celebrations you could have?

OVERCOMING

TODAY'S PROMISE

Because the Sovereign LORD helps me, I will not be disgraced. Therefore, I have set my face like a stone, determined to do his will. And I know that I will not be put to shame.   —ISAIAH 50:7

TODAY'S THOUGHT

As long as you live on this earth, you will never be free from trouble, but you can have the power to overcome it. When you desire and allow the Holy Spirit to work in you, he will help you overcome. When you begin to see the obstacles in your life as opportunities for God to show his power, they will not seem so overwhelming. The hardships and weaknesses that frighten you may be the tools God wants to use to help you overcome.

TODAY'S PLAN

Are you allowing the Holy Spirit to turn your obstacles into his opportunities?

BLESSING OTHERS

TODAY'S PROMISE

As a result of your ministry, they will give glory to God. For your generosity to them and to all believers will prove that you are obedient to the Good News of Christ. And they will pray for you with deep affection because of the overflowing grace God has given to you. —2 CORINTHIANS 9:13-14

TODAY'S THOUGHT

As a river flows freely through an unblocked channel, so the grace and blessing of God flow through you when you follow his ways. When you obey God, your life becomes an open channel for his love and mercy to flow through to others.

TODAY'S PLAN

How well are God's love and mercy flowing through you to others?

APPRECIATION

TODAY'S PROMISE

Give thanks to the LORD, for he is good! His faithful love endures forever. —1 CHRONICLES 16:34

TODAY'S THOUGHT

We pray often when we have a need. We pray often when we want something from God. But what happens when God answers prayer? Do we remember to pray as often and as fervently in thanking him for answered prayer? When we understand God's awesome splendor, overwhelming power, and extravagant grace, we appreciate more and more the privilege of forgiveness and fellowship with him.

TODAY'S PLAN

Check up on yourself to see how thankful you are for answered prayer.

SALVATION

TODAY'S PROMISE

If you confess with your mouth that Jesus is Lord and believe in your heart that God raised him from the dead, you will be saved. —ROMANS 10:9

TODAY'S THOUGHT

If you believe that Jesus saves you from sin, confess your sins to him, and acknowledge that he is Lord of all, then you are a new person inside. Sin will no longer control you, and you are guaranteed eternal life in heaven. Jesus is your Savior and Lord. How do you know? Because God promised, and God always keeps his promises. Although your relationship with Jesus as the Savior and Lord of your life begins at a moment in time, you should have an active, daily trust in Jesus Christ that continues throughout your life.

TODAY'S PLAN

Do you truly believe?

THANKFULNESS

TODAY'S PROMISE

Since everything God created is good, we should not reject any of it but receive it with thanks. —1 TIMOTHY 4:4

TODAY'S THOUGHT

A spirit of gratitude and praise changes the way you look at life. Complaining connects you to your unhappiness—gratitude and praise connect you to the source of real joy. When you make thanksgiving a regular part of your life, you stay focused on all God has done and continues to do for you.

TODAY'S PLAN

What can you do to begin developing an attitude of thankfulness?

THANKFULNESS

TODAY'S PROMISE

Be thankful in all circumstances, for this is God's will for you who belong to Christ Jesus.

—1 THESSALONIANS 5:18

TODAY'S THOUGHT

A loving spouse works hard all day at the office or at home. Do you bother to say thanks? Think about how often in a day someone does something for you, however small. Do you remember to thank those people? Now think about how often God helps you in life. Think about how much God has given you. When you pause to thank God, you recognize that he has a track record of blessing you, providing for you, and protecting you. How often do you say thanks to him? Giving thanks is a way to celebrate both the gift and the giver. Thank him often!

TODAY'S PLAN

When was the last time you thanked God for the blessings in your life?

TRUSTING GOD

TODAY'S PROMISE

God has given both his promise and his oath. These two things are unchangeable because it is impossible for God to lie. Therefore, we who have fled to him for refuge can have great confidence as we hold to the hope that lies before us. —HEBREWS 6:18

TODAY'S THOUGHT

God cannot lie because he is truth. In other words, he doesn't have to work at being truthful because truth is the very essence of God's DNA. He doesn't have a sinful nature that corrupts the truth in him. Therefore, God cannot lie and cannot break his promises. Everything he says is true and will never change. So God can be trusted for your hope of being sinless someday because he alone conquered death by raising Jesus from the dead. Your hope is that, like Jesus, you will be raised as he was to live eternally in a perfect heaven.

TODAY'S PLAN

Could you do a better job of trusting that God's Word is true?

PRIORITIES

TODAY'S PROMISE

Jesus replied, "The most important commandment is this: 'You must love the Lord your God with all your heart, all your soul, all your mind, and all your strength.' The second is equally important: 'Love your neighbor as yourself.' No other commandment is greater than these." —MARK 12:29-31

TODAY'S THOUGHT

When the phone rings, most of us will get up to answer it, or at least check the caller ID, because interruptions tend to become top priorities. Our lives usually skip from one urgent interruption to another, and all the while we keep missing what is most important. How can we distinguish true priorities from false ones, like the ringing phone? Jesus clearly stated the two greatest priorities for every person— to love God and to love others. When you sincerely love God, you will also love others.

TODAY'S PLAN

What would your closest friend say are your top two priorities?

SECURITY

TODAY'S PROMISE

Those who trust in the LORD are as secure as Mount Zion; they will not be defeated but will endure forever.

—PSALM 125:1

TODAY'S THOUGHT

Feeling truly secure begins with trusting in God's unfailing love and consistent character. If you choose to believe his promises, then your response should be to obey him, for you will be confident that your life is secure in the hands of God. Nothing can stand against his power, and his power is dedicated to helping those who love him.

TODAY'S PLAN

How can you feel more secure in the arms of God?

COURAGE

TODAY'S PROMISE

I hold you by your right hand—I, the LORD your God. And I say to you, "Don't be afraid. I am here to help you."

—ISAIAH 41:13

TODAY'S THOUGHT

We are naturally afraid when we walk alone in frightening places and circumstances. But we have more courage when we walk with a friend who is strong. With the Lord God, who holds the universe in his hands, we should feel free to be courageous. Consider what comforts us when we face the death of a loved one. Flowers, food, even the words of others help, but a greater source of strength is our friends and family staying near us, giving us gentle touches and looks that communicate their care. When we face troubled times, we must never forget that God remains close by. This gives us the courage to go on.

TODAY'S PLAN

How can you depend more on God for the courage you need in frightening times?

DECEMBER

FORGIVENESS

TODAY'S PROMISE

If you forgive those who sin against you, your heavenly Father will forgive you. But if you refuse to forgive others, your Father will not forgive your sins.

—MATTHEW 6:14-15

TODAY'S THOUGHT

Being unwilling to forgive others shows that you have not understood or benefited from God's forgiveness, because forgiveness is motivated by unconditional love. When God forgives you, you are freed from guilt and restored to fellowship with him. When you forgive someone who has wronged you, you are free from bitterness and resentment that can saturate your soul like toxic waste. When you have been forgiven by another, you are free from indebtedness to that person. Receiving God's forgiveness and forgiving others are at the core of what it means to be a Christian.

TODAY'S PLAN

Who can you forgive who has hurt you deeply?

ANGELS

Don't forget to show hospitality to strangers, for some who have done this have entertained angels without realizing it! —HEBREWS 13:2

TODAY'S THOUGHT

Angels are God's special messengers who some-times intervene on earth to bring God's justice, to carry out God's will, or to take care of us. Angels play a special role for God both on earth and in heaven. In fact, angels play a greater part in your life than you may realize. Make sure your actions would help rather than hinder the work of angels on earth.

TODAY'S PLAN

Knowing angels may be involved in your life, how will that affect the way you act today?

BROKENNESS

[The Lord says,] "Don't tear your clothing in your grief, but tear your hearts instead." Return to the LORD your God, for he is merciful and compassionate, slow to get angry and filled with unfailing love. He is eager to relent and not punish.

—JOEL 2:13

TODAY'S THOUGHT

When you turn to God in brokenness over your sin, he begins to heal and restore you. God promises to draw close to you when you are brokenhearted about sin in your life.

TODAY'S PLAN

Has your heart been broken over your sin?

CHRISTLIKENESS

TODAY'S PROMISE

[Jesus said,] "I have given you an example to follow. Do as I have done to you." —JOHN 13:15

TODAY'S THOUGHT

Jesus Christ is the ultimate example of someone living to please God. To follow his example doesn't necessarily mean to be a traveling preacher and do miracles; instead, it means to think his thoughts, show his attitudes, and live as he would live. This is an awesome goal, and since you are not perfect, it will be difficult. The key is not in your ability to be perfect but in allowing Jesus Christ to live his perfect life through you.

TODAY'S PLAN

How can you be more like Jesus today?

APPROVAL

TODAY'S PROMISE

There is only one God, and he makes people right with himself only by faith. —ROMANS 3:30

TODAY'S THOUGHT

You receive God's approval by believing that Jesus Christ is God's only Son and that he died on the cross to pay for your sins so that you can have eternal life in heaven with him. There is nothing you need to do—except come to him! This is a gift you should never forget to enjoy and appreciate.

TODAY'S PLAN

Have you taken the step of faith that brings God's approval forever?

GENEROSITY

Wherever your treasure is, there the desires of your heart will also be. —MATTHEW 6:21

Who is more generous—a billionaire who gives one million dollars to his church, or a poor single mom who gives ten dollars? If you have a lot of money, does that mean you are not generous? Jesus said we can't know the answer to those questions without knowing the heart of the giver. Throughout the Bible, God doesn't focus on how much money you have but on how generous you are with it. One thing is clear: Wherever your money goes reveals what you care most about. When you realize that everything you have is a gift from a generous God, it motivates you to share your possessions more freely.

How might generous giving on your part have an impact on the lives of those around you?

EMOTIONS

TODAY'S PROMISE

The Holy Spirit produces this kind of fruit in our lives: love, joy, peace, patience, kindness, goodness, faithfulness, gentleness, and self-control.

—GALATIANS 5:22-23

TODAY'S THOUGHT

We often think of emotions in a negative sense, when they get out of control. But without emotions you cannot experience the power and deep satisfaction of a relationship with God, nor can you live out the character of God. Don't deny your emotions, but don't let them control you or cause you to sin. Use the emotions God has given you to deepen your relationship with him, and you will experience the drama and power of true Christian living. This will have a profound impact on those you serve.

TODAY'S PLAN

What emotions do you have most often that can lead you to a deeper relationship with God?

HOLINESS

TODAY'S PROMISE

I entrust you to God and the message of his grace that is able to build you up and give you an inheritance with all those he has set apart for himself.

—ACTS 20:32

TODAY'S THOUGHT

Holiness means being set apart by God for a specific purpose. You are meant to be different from the rest of the world, and in your life journey, you work to become a little more pure and sinless each day. If you strive to be holy in your earthly life, you will one day arrive at your final destination to stand holy before God.

TODAY'S PLAN

Would others say your life is "set apart" from the way the world wants you to live?

LOVE

TODAY'S PROMISE

[Jesus said,] "When you obey my commandments, you remain in my love. . . . I have told you these things so that you will be filled with my joy. Yes, your joy will overflow!" —JOHN 15:10-11

TODAY'S THOUGHT

Obedience is one important way to express your love for God. This should not be confused with earning God's love by doing good works. You obey God because you are *already* loved, not in order to be loved. As you obey, you will experience increasing joy, because you will see God at work in your life every day.

TODAY'S PLAN

What small step of obedience can you take right now?

FAITH STORIES

TODAY'S PROMISE

Remember the things I have done in the past. For I alone am God! I am God, and there is none like me.

—ISAIAH 46:9

TODAY'S THOUGHT

God wanted his people to remember the past so that they would constantly be aware of his mercy and his power. This produces an attitude of thanksgiving and worship and a confident hope for the future. What is the history of your relationship with God? Can you put into words what he has done for you? Remembering and telling your faith stories of the past is a way to encourage you to greater obedience and trust.

TODAY'S PLAN

With whom can you share the story of your spiritual journey?

December 11

CELEBRATION

Sing for joy, O heavens! Rejoice, O earth! Burst into song, O mountains! For the LORD has comforted his people and will have compassion on them in their suffering.

—ISAIAH 49:13

TODAY'S THOUGHT

God gives you the ultimate reason to celebrate because he has rescued you from the consequences of sin, promises to comfort you in suffering, and guarantees the wonders of eternity. Celebration is a powerful way to increase your hope because it takes your focus off your troubles and puts it on God's current blessings and future promises. Those who love him truly have the most to celebrate!

TODAY'S PLAN

What blessings from God can you celebrate today?

GIFTS

TODAY'S PROMISE

God loved the world so much that he gave his one and only Son, so that everyone who believes in him will not perish but have eternal life. —JOHN 3:16

TODAY'S THOUGHT

The greatest gift God gives you is his Son. Through Jesus, he also gives you the gift of eternal life. What makes the gift so wonderful is that you don't have to work for it or earn it. You simply believe that this is actually happening to you—an offer of eternal life with a perfect God who wants to be your friend for eternity. Then you accept the offer, no one can take it away.

TODAY'S PLAN

With whom can you share a free gift as wonderful as this?

DECEMBER 13

PROBLEMS

TODAY'S PROMISE

Joyful are those who have the God of Israel as their helper, whose hope is in the LORD their God.

—PSALM 146:5

TODAY'S THOUGHT

Problems are opportunities for you to experience God's help. When problems arise unexpectedly, they can cause you to become discouraged, lose hope, feel sorry for yourself, or forget God's promises. At those times it's helpful to remember God's faithfulness in the past, which helps you trust him today and for the future. Remembering what God has done for you ignites the fire of hope and drives away the darkness of despair. You must be willing to look away from your problems long enough to see God's hand reaching out to help you.

TODAY'S PLAN

How do you respond when problems catch you off guard? What memories of God's help in the past inspire your hope the most?

POWER OF GOD

TODAY'S PROMISE

With God's help we will do mighty things.

—PSALM 60:12

TODAY'S THOUGHT

Try not to look at the size of the problem but at the size of your God. When there are great things to be done, you have a great God who will do them through you.

TODAY'S PLAN

How can you rely more on God's power?

DECEMBER 15

REST

It is a permanent sign of my covenant with the people of Israel. For in six days the LORD made heaven and earth, but on the seventh day he stopped working and was refreshed. —EXODUS 31:17

TODAY'S THOUGHT

Why would the omnipotent God of the universe rest following his work of creation? Surely, it wasn't because the Almighty was physically tired! The clue is that God, in ceasing from his work, called his day of rest "holy." God knew you would need to cease from your work to care for your spiritual needs. Work is good, but it must be balanced by regular attention to worship and the health of your soul. God promises your soul will be refreshed if you carve out regular times for worship and spiritual nourishment.

TODAY'S PLAN

Are you resting enough?

SACRIFICE

TODAY'S PROMISE

Everyone who has given up houses or brothers or sisters or father or mother or children or property, for my sake, will receive a hundred times as much in return and will inherit eternal life. —MATTHEW 19:29

TODAY'S THOUGHT

Following Jesus may mean you have to sacrifice a comfortable life. It may mean, if you are forced to declare ultimate loyalty to someone, having to choose to be loyal to Jesus over any other relationships. But Jesus promises to reward such faithful commitment. Your salvation is evident in what you are willing to give up in order to gain a relationship with him.

TODAY'S PLAN

What kinds of sacrifices are you willing to make to follow Jesus?

DECEMBER 17

WEARINESS

Even youths will become weak and tired, and young men will fall in exhaustion. But those who trust in the LORD will find new strength. They will soar high on wings like eagles. They will run and not grow weary. They will walk and not faint.

—ISAIAH 40:30-31

TODAY'S THOUGHT

The Lord will give you renewed strength when you grow weary. When you come to him in praise, he refreshes your heart. When you come to him in prayer, he refreshes your soul. When you come to him in solitude, he refreshes your body. When you come to him in need, he refreshes your mind. When you come to him with thankfulness, he refreshes your perspective. Doing these things releases the burdens of life and draws strength from the One who is the source of strength.

TODAY'S PLAN

Are you ready to rely more on God and discover the benefits of his spiritual strength?

SERVICE

TODAY'S PROMISE

[Jesus said,] "Now I am giving you a new commandment: Love each other. Just as I have loved you, you should love each other. Your love for one another will prove to the world that you are my disciples."

—JOHN 13:34-35

TODAY'S THOUGHT

Regardless of the level of your gifts and abilities, God expects you to invest what he's given you in the lives of others. He promises that when you follow Christ's loving example, you too will become an example of his love to the world, and your example will change the way many live.

TODAY'S PLAN

What can you do to serve someone today?

DECEMBER 19

PURITY

TODAY'S PROMISE

Who may climb the mountain of the LORD? Who may stand in his holy place? Only those whose hands and hearts are pure.

—PSALM 24:3-4

TODAY'S THOUGHT

Purity comes from a desire to be like Jesus in your thought, words, and actions. Although you can never be fully free of sin in this life, you can strive for that. God promises to honor and bless those who strive for pure hearts, because it demonstrates a sincere commitment to be like Jesus.

TODAY'S PLAN

Are you striving for purity each day?

RISK

TODAY'S PROMISE

Mary responded, "I am the Lord's servant. May everything you have said about me come true." And then the angel left her. —LUKE 1:38

TODAY'S THOUGHT

When God asks you to follow him, he rarely gives all the information right away about what is going to happen. When you walk in faith, he gives guidance as you go. Mary risked her marriage, her reputation, and her future by becoming the mother of Jesus. Take the risk of doing things God's way. It is not without risks, but God's rewards far outweigh the risks.

TODAY'S PLAN

What risks do you need to take in following God?

GIFTS

TODAY'S PROMISE

A spiritual gift is given to each of us so we can help each other. . . . It is the one and only Spirit who distributes all these gifts. He alone decides which gift each person should have. —1 CORINTHIANS 12:7, 11

TODAY'S THOUGHT

When we find the perfect gift for a friend or loved one, it gives us great joy to see that person use and delight in it. Similarly, God hand-picks special gifts for each one of us, and he takes great delight when we use those gifts for his glory. Some are "spiritual gifts," abilities he has given especially to each individual. You never use up these spiritual gifts; rather, the more you use them, the more they grow and allow you to make a unique contribution in your sphere of influence. They are a symbol of God's deep, personal, and attentive love and commitment to you.

TODAY'S PLAN

What spiritual gift has God given you? How will you use it?

PEACE

TODAY'S PROMISE

A child is born to us, a son is given to us. The government will rest on his shoulders. And he will be called: Wonderful Counselor, Mighty God, Everlasting Father, Prince of Peace. His government and its peace will never end. He will rule with fairness and justice from the throne of his ancestor David for all eternity. The passionate commitment of the LORD of Heaven's Armies will make this happen!
—ISAIAH 9:6-7

TODAY'S THOUGHT

Lasting peace comes only from Jesus Christ, the Prince of Peace. His rule over all creation ensures it. When Christ has control of your heart, he gives you the peace of mind that comes from knowing that your life is in the hands of a loving God who is passionately committed to you.

TODAY'S PLAN

Do you search for peace within yourself or from the Prince of Peace?

MIGHTY GOD

TODAY'S PROMISE

The Mighty One is holy, and he has done great things for me. . . . His mighty arm has done tremendous things!

—LUKE 1:49-51

The Son radiates God's own glory and expresses the very character of God, and he sustains everything by the mighty power of his command.

—HEBREWS 1:3

TODAY'S THOUGHT

It's hard to picture the baby Jesus as the mighty God, but he was mighty enough to create the world, live a sinless life, heal countless people, calm storms, and conquer death. He is mighty enough to conquer your troubles too!

TODAY'S PLAN

Do you see Jesus more as meek and lowly or as a mighty warrior?

GOD'S TIMING

When we were utterly helpless, Christ came at just the right time and died for us sinners. —ROMANS 5:6

The Hebrew people had been longing for the Messiah for centuries, yet God sent Jesus to earth at just the right time. You may not fully understand why this was perfect timing until you get to heaven and see God's complete plan, but you can be assured that God sent Jesus at the time when the most people would be reached with the good news of salvation, both present and future.

Where has God's perfect timing been evident in your life?

SALVATION

TODAY'S PROMISE

The Savior—yes, the Messiah, the Lord—has been born today in Bethlehem, the city of David! And you will recognize him by this sign: You will find a baby wrapped snugly in strips of cloth, lying in a manger.

—LUKE 2:11-12

TODAY'S THOUGHT

God often accomplishes his purposes in unexpected ways. Maybe that is why he chose to have Jesus born in a stable rather than a palace, why he chose tiny Bethlehem rather than the city of Jerusalem, and why the news of Jesus' birth went first to shepherds rather than to kings. God may have done all this to show that life's greatest gift—salvation through Jesus—is available to all. It may also show that the lowly and humble might have a better chance of receiving that message, living by it, and even leading by it.

TODAY'S PLAN

Have you accepted life's greatest gift?

NEEDS

TODAY'S PROMISE

Your Father knows exactly what you need even before you ask him! . . . Your heavenly Father already knows all your needs. —MATTHEW 6:8, 32

TODAY'S THOUGHT

Learning to recognize the difference between needs and wants allows you to find contentment in living God's way. The more you focus on what God values, the more you will be able to distinguish your wants from your needs. If you constantly feel discontented, you may be focusing more on what you want than on what God knows you most need.

TODAY'S PLAN

Could you be satisfied if God gave you only what you needed and not what you wanted? Can you trust that this might be best for you?

DECEMBER 27

HEAVEN

TODAY'S PROMISE

There is more than enough room in my Father's home. If this were not so, would I have told you that I am going to prepare a place for you? —JOHN 14:2

TODAY'S THOUGHT

Not only is there a heaven, but Jesus is making preparations for your arrival. Heaven is described most often in terms of being your home. It is not a paradise you will simply visit on vacation; it is an eternal dwelling place where you will live in joyful fellowship with your heavenly Father and his family.

TODAY'S PLAN

Do you live as if heaven is a reality? How might your actions change if you did?

ETERNITY

TODAY'S PROMISE

Calling the crowd to join his disciples, he said, "If any of you wants to be my follower, you must turn from your selfish ways, take up your cross, and follow me. If you try to hang on to your life, you will lose it. But if you give up your life for my sake and for the sake of the Good News, you will save it." —MARK 8:34-35

TODAY'S THOUGHT

When you are absolutely convinced that Jesus died on the cross to spare you from eternal punishment and give you the gift of eternal life, the troubles of this world are put into perspective. You know that your future—for all eternity— is secure. Then you begin to understand how God intended you to live, and you become more willing to "give up" those things that gratify only you and pursue those things that make a difference to God and others.

TODAY'S PLAN

Can you learn to forgo your own agenda for God's agenda for you?

LOOKING AHEAD

TODAY'S PROMISE

Take delight in the LORD, and he will give you your heart's desires.
—PSALM 37:4

TODAY'S THOUGHT

As you think about goals for the coming year, a good place to begin is with a commitment to apply your faith to everyday life and to become more confident in what you believe. When you adopt these goals, many other issues in your life will fall in line, because there will be no conflict between what you do and what you believe.

TODAY'S PLAN

How often do you have a conflict between what you know you should do and what you actually do? What can you do to have that conflict less often?

FOLLOWING

TODAY'S PROMISE

The LORD says, "I will guide you along the best pathway for your life. I will advise you and watch over you."

—PSALM 32:8

TODAY'S THOUGHT

Those who want to follow God often take a very different path from those who follow someone else. God promises great reward to those who follow him. If you want to follow God, go where he leads. Stay close enough to keep your eyes focused on him. That will ensure that you will go in whatever direction he leads.

TODAY'S PLAN

Are you staying close enough to God to see where he is leading you?

ENDURANCE

TODAY'S PROMISE

When your faith remains strong through many trials, it will bring you much praise and glory and honor on the day when Jesus Christ is revealed to the whole world.
                                                            —1 PETER 1:7

TODAY'S THOUGHT

The greatest reward for finishing a life well is eternal life with God. This reward is given to all who endure the challenges of living faithfully for him—persecution, ridicule, and other temptations. Just as marathoners train hard and build up their endurance to finish the race well, so Christians must train and build up endurance to live a life of faith in Jesus and stay strong to the end. When your endurance is strong and fit, you will not collapse during the race. You will push on toward the goal of becoming more and more like Jesus until you cross the finish line into heaven and receive the eternal rewards he has promised.

TODAY'S PLAN

What are you doing to develop your spiritual endurance?

TOPICAL INDEX

SCRIPTURE INDEX

Do-able. <u>Daily.</u> Devotions.

IT'S EASY TO GROW WITH GOD THE ONE YEAR WAY.

The One Year Mini for Women helps women connect with God through several Scripture verses and a devotional thought. Perfect for use anytime and anywhere between regular devotion times. Hardcover.

The One Year Mini for Students offers students from high school through college a quick devotional connection with God anytime and anywhere. Stay grounded through the ups and downs of a busy student lifestyle. Hardcover.

The One Year Mini for Moms provides encouragement and affirmation for those moments during a mom's busy day when she needs to be reminded of the high value of her role. Hardcover.

The One Year Mini for Busy Women is for women who don't have time to get it all done but need to connect with God during the day. Hardcover.

The One Year Mini for Men helps men connect with God anytime, anywhere between their regular devotion times through Scripture quotations and a related devotional thought. Hardcover.

The One Year Mini for Leaders motivates and inspires leaders to maximize their God-given leadership potential using scriptural insights. Hardcover.